# THE ESCAPE ARTIST

The Escape Artist
Copyright © 2026 by Ian Jarvis

All rights reserved under the Pan-American and International Copyright Conventions. This book may not be reproduced in whole or in part, except for brief quotations embodied in critical articles or reviews, in any form or by any means, electronic or mechanical, including photocopying, recording, or by any information storage and retrieval system now known or hereinafter invented, without written permission of the publisher.

ISBN (paperback): 978-1-968919-11-5
ISBN (ebook): 978-1-968919-12-2

Armin Lear Press, Inc.
215 W Riverside Drive, #4362
Estes Park, CO 80517

# THE ESCAPE ARTIST

## IAN JARVIS

*This book is dedicated to my wife, Lisa, who was born with courage, and to my daughter, who found it.*

*I don't believe there's a bearded guy in heaven, sitting on a gold chair, playing pinball with our lives. I do believe there are magical forces circling this planet that sometimes intervene.*

*I know this because they have saved my ass more times than I deserve.*

Ian Jarvis

# CONTENTS

| | | |
|---|---|---|
| 1 | Out To Sea | 1 |
| 2 | *Kilu* | 13 |
| 3 | Nice Jewish Boy From New Jersey | 23 |
| 4 | Lights On – Losing It in Provincetown | 29 |
| 5 | Georgetown University | 43 |
| 6 | The Acid Test | 53 |
| 7 | The Summer of Love | 59 |
| 8 | Down and Out in Marrakesh and Tangier | 65 |
| 9 | Runner | 87 |
| 10 | Future Ex-Wife | 99 |
| 11 | Living Dangerously in Corsica | 113 |
| 12 | Let Louche in Paris | 121 |
| 13 | The Return | 135 |
| 14 | Deliverance | 147 |

# 1
# OUT TO SEA

Alice Schroth had just turned fifty-eight the night her Cadillac Eldorado took a feathered slide off a slick, Ohio highway. She died hypothermic, at the foot of a tree. The Schroth estate, nearly two million dollars, passed to adopted son, Rick, a college sophomore who took a semester off to grieve but became a junkie instead. Generous to a fault, he eventually turned most of his friends into addicts but no one saw that coming the night we met at his Cincinnati duplex: Rick's wedding party, his idea of celebration, an intro to the exotic bird, heroin.

Cinci was new to the drug revolution, pinching in from the two coasts like an army of ants. The city had been a trading post on the banks of the Ohio river when a canal connected it to the Mississippi in 1825. Prosperity came fast, and the newly rich moved up to Mount Adams for better air, quiet nights and a stunning view across the big river to Covington, Kentucky; lawless, welcoming of whores and gambling, where Cinci's wealthy went to play.

Rick had moved to Mount Adams too. We were on his patio, checking out the view when he called us to his bedroom, lined with gurgling lava lamps and red, velvet curtains. Alone on a sofa sat his bride, Missy, a wisp of a girl, her wedding dress clutched to her knees, watching her husband, whose silky blond hair cascaded past his shoulders, mix two batches of brown powder in a mortar and pestle. Missy was a blueblood from Louisville, Kentucky. She'd said, "Yes" to Rick's proposal because she didn't know how to say, "No," but she wasn't having any part of this.

Rick, immune to disapproval, tasted a pinch of his powder, smiled, and motioned us forward. One by one he tied us off. One by one he boiled a dose on a small spoon, then spiked a vein, and when a crimson cloud slow rolled up the dropper, he squeezed his corrosive brew into our hearts and minds. We were fine, Strawberry Fields fine, until our host decided to tweak the mix for me, the new guy, in from San Francisco on a half-ton Chevy. Rick cooked up a custom dose, ran his finger softly over my forearm, found a spot and pushed the plunger, a bullet to the brain.

"Click."

I became an accidental astronaut.

"Click."

I looked at Rick.

"Click."

He shrunk to the size of a pin.

"Click"

He disappeared.

They said I hit the floor like an epileptic. I was dragged upstairs, slapped around, dumped in a cold shower until I came to. I was twenty-one, I went back to party unmarked by my two-step with death. I shot up five, maybe six times that winter, but the last hit wasn't an overdose, it was a bad dose, puking and shitting so long I swore I'd never buy another bag if I could just feel better. That all-nighter punched my card for heroin. I was done. Most of Rick's friends ended up ruined or dead.

Shooting smack had one upside: an exit strategy for Vietnam. This war wasn't some overarching battle with world evil, it was a depressing, corrupt, political play that had already sent forty thousand kids home in body bags. Vietnam was the first American crusade where blood and blown limbs were screened in real time, so this sacrifice didn't have the balm of national unity. Volunteers were hard to come by and to cover their losses, the military cut standards, zeroed out college exemptions, and drafted almost every man they could find.

Well almost. If you had the right doctor, there were medical loopholes like heel spurs or heart problems. Drug addicts and gays, criminals of the first order, were tossed too. Everyone else, mostly blacks and working-class whites, got a year in the jungle, hollowed out like an anthill. I didn't want a twelve-month waltz with the draft board over my commitment to non-violence so when Uncle Sam called, I moved to Vermont and rented a barn for $25 a month. I worked on cars downstairs, slept in the large loft above, and a month later, began prepping for the draft; amphetamine this time, ten days mainlining, morning, noon, and night.

In the long run, crystal meth will shred your heart and turn your teeth to sand but in the short run it's an amazing high, percolating with optimism and sex. On the first hit, seconds after shooting up, hard with heat, I fast-fucked girlfriend Janice, behind a big, Marshall amp—my idea of discretion since I had friends in the room. Minutes later, decompressed, high as a kite, heart in overtime, I passed out while pissing from the hay loft, bounced off a barbed wire fence twenty feet below and broke—nothing. I walked back in the barn with just a cut on my chest and a ripped shirt. Who's going to argue that kind of luck when there's a war going on? Who's going to question what you deserve?

Last night on speed, the hallucinations took over. I watched a battalion of leggy bugs swarming out of a cut on my thigh and I, sheriff of my own body, grabbed a razor blade and went after them; would have gotten every one of the fuckers too, but Janice woke up, saw the three-inch circle of pulp I'd carved in my flesh, the blood pooled on the floor, she pulled the blade, and dragged me to bed.

At eight that morning, a warm, sunny, winter is finally over morning, I, filthy, long haired and bug eyed, set out to meet my maker over Vietnam. I walked onto the US Army bus parked on Main Street in Montpellier, filled with excited, fresh-faced, young Vermonters ready to do anything but go back to the farm. Standing tall in my jean jacket, the word, "Nico" stenciled on it, I waited while their conversation, the chatter, ground to a halt, caught a pair of eyes and said, "Don't fuck with me . . . and I won't fuck with you."

I sat at the rear and looked up at the giant sign of Chief Pontiac on the rooftop of Cody's Pontiac and Chevrolet. The Chief was rusty, his war paint faded, the neon broken; all that was left of America's once-upon-a-time when everyone knew what they were getting, once-upon-a-time when our fathers walked into car showrooms and ordered the new model without even seeing it because they were Chevy guys or Ford guys and there were no recalls and their joy in those shiny, chrome-plated new cars was palpable; no debit cards or interest rates or weak chinned assholes in the back creating lease plans that looked good but weren't.

Chief Pontiac wasn't watching over General Motors now. Detroit had knocked off this symbol of purity and power while dumping their slag in the countryside under a gentleman's agreement that kept the truth tucked away, that made the press play nice so a guy like John or Bobby Kennedy could fuck Marilyn Monroe in plain sight, and no one said word one, so that women would stay home, and children would be born and it looked perfect, but deep inside where I could never articulate it, I knew, though they told us otherwise, that putting my head under a desk in elementary school would not keep the atomic bomb at bay.

Our bus coughed up a cloud of black smoke and headed south to the Official, United States Army Induction Center in Manchester, New Hampshire, a state that had just changed its motto to, "Live Free or Die." We took Route 7, a three-hour drive through low hills, small mountains, past rocky farms and skinny cows. Because US Army inspections began at 6 AM, all the Vermont draftees spent the night before in a cheap, Manchester motel, a sleepover that might have slowed me down except Janice drove in with more drugs to keep the magic alive and I showed up for the roll call, high and fragile, committed to a goal, with no plan. They put us in a windowless basement with fluorescent lights, shiny green walls and army issue metal tables. We milled around while kids made dumb jokes, then I heard some uniform say,

"They assassinated Robert Kennedy last night."

I had played with Kennedy's children, swum in his pool, dipped myself in his light and power and energy, and because I was half gone I burst into tears and reconnected to Robert and Ethel and John and Robert Jr. and spilled my shock and anger in a raging speech which – and somewhere inside I knew exactly what I was doing – hit my first marker to the holy grail for thousands of eighteen year olds; a US Army 4-F rating, the game winning rejection that would keep us out of uniform unless a battalion of Commies were sailing up the Potomac.

"America the beautiful?" I shouted. "Fuck me, that's who killed Kennedy, you killed him your fucking machine killed him just like it killed his brother. Who's next? Who's this stupid, insane war serve? Tell me you idiots, tell me who this serves, just tell me that for Chrissake and then I'll go kill people in pajamas and straw hats, I will kill them if you just tell me why Bobby Kennedy is fucking dead!"

They walked me to a corner, left me alone, then took us across the street to a big, grey, Federal building fronted by four, wide, Greek columns. Inside, a large room was filled with chairs for a short, written test. Half an hour later, everyone else had come and gone, but I was still staring at the math section. A bull-necked sergeant walked over. "Come on, Tarzan," he said, yanking me off the seat. "It's time for your physical." In the locker room, I stayed on message; after ten, slack-jawed minutes unbuttoning my shirt, they told me to keep my pants on. At the hearing eval, I pressed every wrong button. I read the eye chart like I was blind. Nice moves, but I wanted a kicker no one could ignore. I found it at the blood test, when the doctor saw the tracks,

"I'll put that needle in my own vein, sir," I said, quite politely, I thought.

He gave me a baleful look, told a private to lock my arm down, then spiked it. I yanked the syringe out, grabbed the soldier's leg, crying for my mother. The guy panicked, tried shaking me off only I was wrapped around his thigh like a dog in heat so we three legged it past a dozen conscripts in tidy whites to a US Army psychiatrist, my target audience, where I could share the tragic path from LSD to speed and heroin. It was a beautiful story, tied to every preconception.

The shrink, a balding, thin-lipped Captain, said, "Looks like you got what you deserved . . ." I couldn't have agreed more. Thirty minutes later I was on the street with an armed forces document listing my achievements:

## DURING THE COURSE OF YOUR PHYSICAL EXAMINATION THE FOLLOWING DEFICIENCIES WERE FOUND.

"Subject is a pre-morbid schizophrenic suffering from post LSD psychosis, uncontrollable visual hallucinations, and paroxysmal fears."

The doctor, not entirely heartless, bonused me a long-term prescription for Thorazine; a heavy-duty tranquilizer, prized on the street. That would be an income stream for months. I went back to Vermont, slept fifteen hours and woke refreshed. It was summertime, soft and leafy, but the sweet season is short in the Green Mountain state, a tease more than a season and anyway, who wanted to live between stunted hills and dirt roads when it would soon get cold enough to freeze deer meat in the noonday sun.

I closed my car repair biz, gave Janice a VW convertible for her return to Cinci and called in Mark Pockros, close friend, acid-swilling dropout. I believe there are maybe ten people, outside of family, we'll know all our life. Everyone else is meant to stay awhile for an exchange of gifts, and move on. Mark and I looked alike, laughed a lot, were high all the time. There was no one I felt closer to. We've had good times and bad, but we are tight to this day.

Mark had just been fired from VISTA, Lyndon Johnson's anti-poverty program, for growing pot in his West Virginia backyard, then fucking a farmer's wife and then the daughter. He capped it by taking a group of adolescent boys to a County Fair where he wrapped up their day at the burlesque tent by throwing $20 onstage and going down on one of the strippers.

VISTA's write up took Mark out of the war. Now that we were both rejected, he wanted a drive to San Francisco. All we had to do was unload the BMW motorcycle I'd shipped from Ibiza, its engine case stuffed with three kilos of hash. It was risky business, but now the hash was sold, the motor rebuilt, so I drove my bike to Boston's, Riverside Motorcycles, left it there on consignment and we split for California.

Mark's bright yellow Buick, bought from his grandmother, didn't have power steering or electric windows, but it was clean and in great shape. We were going to drive cross country in three days, just like the thousands of tattooed cowboys hauling America's industrial output coast to coast on 18-wheelers, their powers pharmaceutically enhanced with prescriptions for what they called, 'Pep Pills.' We snorted our amphetamine in the back seat and nicked past their thumping diesels like a hornet.

Mark had a friend in San Francisco. We would stay there and in return I'd swap out a broken engine in the guy's truck. We slept on the floor of his apartment despite my prized skills. The couch belonged to a skinny vegetarian who'd stopped using drugs after discovering ginseng was both healthy and a great high. Pretty cool, until he decided he could mainline the extract for better effect. "I knew I was in trouble," he said, "when my arm went numb." He spent two days in an ICU.

San Francisco looks nice in photos; sunny blue skies, old fashioned trolleys, charming houses on the hills, but I couldn't connect there. A dense fog rolled in most mornings, the ocean was icy, the people too. Alcatraz stood in the bay like a missile base minding its own business, which summed the whole place up for me, so when I finished the engine job, I drifted to Berkeley across the bridge; low key, smiling, open-faced neighbors and the vigorous, University of California with 25,000 eager students.

The town had lost its way a few years before, when the entire school was shut down by students rioting for Free Speech, a movement that had more to do with the war in Vietnam than the first amendment. It didn't take long for the UC administration to cave and when it all went to hell, California's old guard returned fire. They promoted Ronald Reagan, B-list actor and spokesperson for Borax soap, to run for governor. Ronnie won with a promise to "Clean up the mess at UCB," Reagan pushed law and order throughout his term and the students went back to their books, but Berkeley's dreamers, artists and acid heads never gave up. For them it was business as usual, no work, social justice, communal living, free love.

That's how I met east coast transplant, Jane Lancaster. I'd always been told badass *shiksas* were out to get our Jewish DNA. For some boys, it's danger that drives discovery; I loved her otherness, blond hair, pale skin, bright blue eyes. I was charmed by an airy naïveté that would have become seriously annoying if we'd spent any time together but a week after I moved in, Riverside Motorcycles called from Boston. They had a buyer for my BMW.

"Great," I said. "Send the money."

"The guy, calls himself Big Sid, wants to trade a sixty-foot schooner for your bike."

"What? Wait . . . wait . . . did you say a boat? A sailboat? A real sailboat?"

Mark flew to Boston to handle negotiations, a least he'd done some sailing. The closest I'd come to crossing open water was the Staten Island ferry. A day later, we owned our dream; *Kilu*, a two-masted schooner built in 1895 to dredge oysters and clams in the Chesapeake Bay. Who, at twenty-one, would have walked away, even if we'd known she'd been raised off Boston Harbor after sinking from neglect and rusted pumps.

As a child, I read countless books about tramp freighters and their outlaw crews. I sat with toy boats in the bathtub and saw yachts at sea. I'd never forgotten Errol Flynn's Captain Blood, swiping Olivia De Havilland from her arrogant Spanish count, a man whose castles and gold couldn't keep his fiancée from handing off her virginity to a handsome swashbuckler on a moonlit night at sea. Hell yes. I would raise a staysail, belay those ropes, know with one weathered look, the currents, wind, and weather. I'd have a woman in every port and the only anchor in my life would be the one I could winch up any given day. My dream about blue skies, nights at the tiller, and open ocean was unsullied by any thought about skills, money, or the kind of weather that could transform zero planning and bad luck into catastrophe and death.

I sold the Buick, took a cheap flight to Vermont via Montreal. Mark would meet me at Burlington airport. Easy trip, until I stepped off the plane. Five lawmen, immaculate, beefy, gun ready, were circled at the base of the steps.

*Wow,* I asked myself. *Who are they waiting for?* Then I saw a stewardess pointing at me. Of course! How could any Air Canadian not tell her pilot that a long hair from the states, wearing an Afghan coat, had boarded the plane? How could he not be carrying, not be ripe for a press-ready confirmation that Canada and Vermont were doing their part in the War on Drugs? They were right. I was holding, only it was a half-ounce of Lebanese hash, not the kilos these guys had in mind. They were gonna be seriously disappointed, but possession, no matter how small, was still a righteous bust. My fifteen grams could put me away for years.

I had seconds to fuck them, just didn't know how. I ambled down the gangway all innocent, all smiles, not one step out of step while the cops closed ranks to give me the news. When they were in my face, a scrum so tight no one could move, I yelled, "What the fuck!" and raised a clenched fist over my head. They panicked, wrestled it down. No one saw my other hand pull the dope out of my pocket and drop it at their feet,

I held my breath while Vermont's finest trampled the evidence, then marched me from the scene of my crime. Minutes later, I was in the terminal. No lining up at customs for Ian, no casual flip through my passport by a highly trained agent trying to stay awake. I was in the express lane, suspect's highway, open for business. It only took a few minutes to paw through my knapsack and sleeping bag. No kilos there. Adjusting horizons, they turned out my pockets, wallet, and sneakers. Fingers were slow walked up my pants and shirt until they had, at least in my mind, looked everywhere. Then someone snapped on a pair of rubber gloves.

"You're not gonna do that . . ." I said.

"Bend over, kid, put your hands on the desk."

When he pulled his finger out of my ass, nothing of note on it, they glumly returned the suspect's possessions. Mark was curb side, air guitaring "Stairway to Heaven." We laughed our asses off, smoked a joint, and drove to Plainfield. My partner was on a roll. First, he bought our nineteenth-century yacht. Now he'd traded thirty tabs of acid for an orange, 1936 Ford pickup whose owner hadn't mentioned the truck's cracked cylinder head. We'd be out of warranty the moment our seller handed over the keys but thirty minutes after startup, the engine would vaporize all cooling water and we 'd come full stop in a cloud of steam, boiled antifreeze and melting rubber.

Fifty miles down the road, that's exactly what happened, only when the temperature gauge redlined, I pulled over before it turned into a catastrophe. Two Jerry cans, twenty gallons of water and four stops later, we made it to Boston's waterfront and found Lewis wharf; a hundred-year-old commercial dock with an empty, two story, stone building, construction material lined up all along its walls. The sharp smell of iodine and creosote hung in the air. Gulls, perched on white spotted pilings, croaked nervously as we passed, our excitement growing as we closed in on our prize; the sixty-five-foot, two masted *Kilu*, rocking gently at wharf's end. We owned this thing!

# 2
# KILU

Up close, my bedtime story about endless pussy became a fright film. She was a hag, a dump, clotted with piles of rotten wood, dead TVs, wallboard, and abandoned furniture. My first step on deck, a nail sticking through a plywood board punctured my boot. I leapt away, made a perfect landing on another nail. The third jump was to the cabin roof where I decided, even though those spikes had been rusty and both feet were bleeding, there was little chance of tetanus.

I limped forward for a face-to-face with the *Kilu's* carved mermaid under the bowsprit. I ran a hand over her Medusa-like hair, faded red lips and bare breasts. From there, the *Kilu's* wide deck and swooping, low freeboard looked sleek and powerful. The raked, twin masts seemed to touch the sky. I imagined her under full sail, beating across a boiling sea, a crew of sure-footed men on deck and atop the rigging, their dark slickers glistening with spray. It was beautiful. I was all in.

Time to roll a joint and explore the accommodations. I opened the hatch, climbed down. She was clean and spacious inside. Thick, hand-hewn wood planks felt strong underfoot. A dozen portholes gave good light. Our "galley" was in name only since there was no gas and the fridge was a true, ice box. The toilet worked perfectly though, emptied everything, right into the bay. There were bunks for ten along the walls but only one private cabin and since we were co-captains, we flipped a coin. Mark won. I was bummed.

Next morning we began clearing the crap on deck. After two days, *Kilu* was cleaned up and we felt great, but when her profile became boat, not barge, the man who sold it to us, Big Sid, all 300 pounds of him, wiggled over to say he could see now that his boat was worth more than he thought.

"Sold it too cheap," he told us, 'I'll need a thousand dollars on top of the BMW."

Sid was a lifetime criminal with a prehensile brain, but he knew from day one he was going take the *Kilu* back or stick us for more money. We weren't handing over our fantasy but we weren't going toe to toe either. We got vague. Sid, very present tense, showed up the next morning with two friends agile enough to kick our ass. He gave us three days to deliver.

We were the only boat on that side of the wharf, no fence, no streetlights, no protection. Kids in the neighborhood, an Italian enclave, were already lining up on a nearby jetty to throw stones at the *Kilu* while screaming, "Get the fuck outta here you dirty hippies!"

. Sid returned as promised but this time he played nice, gave us another week. We didn't know how to protect ourselves or get this asshole off our back. We bought a shotgun which I slept with because Mark had the stateroom, and I was under the hatch. Our deadline was coming. We had no idea how that would go. Then, in a halo of perfect timing, we stepped off the *Kilu* one day at sunset and met a red-haired kid our age whose architect father was the new owner of Lewis Wharf.

The son, John Naughton Jr., was interested in our old boat. We took him on tour, hung out below. Eventually talk turned to Big Sid. John commiserated and went home, but the next day, he told us we could berth the *Kilu* on the other side of the wharf at no charge. They had million-dollar yachts there, running water, electricity, barbed wire, it was heaven. Since our motor wasn't working, John's dad had also given his son permission to bring the family's forty-foot yawl around that night to tow us over

Near 10 PM, we heard the soft chug of an engine, John's boat, lights off, was ghosting out of the dark. We were wary, didn't know if Big Sid or his people were watching. Mark and I crept topside, quietly undid the lines and tied on to his stern. No one stepped from the shadows, no shouts echoed over the bay. We slowly edged out of our berth and around the head of the wharf to our slip in the new world.

*Kilu* had ridden the tides for years. Now, she was alive, gliding across the water, making a wake, a breeze in our faces! John's boat turned to go round the head of the wharf. Mark spun the wheel to follow. That's when we found out the Kilu, on top of its dead engine, also had no rudder! John's boat went one way. ours went the other. The rope parted and our sixty-footer became a ten-ton battering ram whose long, oak bowsprit was heading right for the harbormaster's cabin, afloat at the entrance. This was the last guy you'd want to wake up by sinking his home. John, on the yawl, 100 feet away, stood transfixed by the train wreck he'd put in motion. We were helpless, but at the last moment I ran up the bowsprit, wrapped my arms around the tip and swung my feet out to land on the side of the cabin. I pushed against the weight of our boat with every muscle. The *Kilu* began to slow, then slow a bit more while the floating cabin gently gave way too. Seconds later, my knees punched back to my shoulders, we were dead in the water. I looked around. The crew stood wide-eyed. John was dancing on his boat in relief. The crash, destruction, lights, people, police, reporters and spectators, all that should have happened, hadn't.

Ten minutes later, the *Kilu* was berthed and secure. In the morning, the paying customers woke to new neighbors. A few of the well-heeled huffed over to confirm that hippies had broken into the reservation. To his credit, Mister Owner of Lewis Wharf held his ground when the phone lit up, so we went to work. I got up every morning, joyful and focused. The yachties saw fourteen-hour days cleaning, painting, and fixing. They watched me pull the engine and rebuild it on deck, saw lights off at a reasonable hour, no clouds of marijuana and not one orgy among the revolutionaries. Over the next weeks, Susan and her boyfriend Alec, came aboard. Two teenaged girls showed up, whose parents didn't seem to mind them spending afternoons with us. Larry, a guy from MIT whose Pontiac convertible had flowers painted all over it, joined up too.

The boat owners got interested, we became part of the gated community. That didn't take care of Big Sid. He was waiting for me outside one day, angry and threatening. He wanted his money or his boat and no rich man's playpen was gonna keep him from getting it. Each morning, I'd poke my head out and look around. I was careful about hitting the street and though we had friends in the marina, we didn't tell them. We thought it might resurrect any reservations they had.

Then one night, drinking in our wheelhouse with Jim, who owned the converted steel trawler berthed directly behind, our story about Big Sid came up. The next day he checked with the cops and confirmed Sid was dangerous. Jim passed the story around the marina. Some of the owners came down on our side, brought guns to their boats. It was like that for a week. I would come on deck and wonder if a shooter was out there. At night, we locked the hatch despite the heat.

The stalemate ended the afternoon Big Sid pulled up on Commonwealth Avenue and shoved me in his Mercedes. He had two characters in the back and our ride had the markers of my last day on earth. I barely spoke, just nodded and listened. Sid made one mistake; he left me on the street with a threat. Said he was Mafia, we had forty-eight hours to bring the money or we were dead.

I knew this guy was capable of serious trouble, but I didn't believe he was Mafia. I told Jim and the next day, he said we'd be getting a visitor. Guy shows up straight out of central casting; thick Boston accent, slick hair, gold chain, piercing eyes, quiet voice. We went below, Mark hiding in the galley with the shotgun. My guest asked for the story. I laid it out. He listened, said, "Okay," and left. Two days later, Big Sid was in the hospital, seriously in the hospital we were told, with broken bones and internal injuries. The Mafia had kicked his ass because you never in your life and not on your life, tell anyone you're one of them when you're not.

We were free. There was nothing between us and our Caribbean dream. Our friends at the marina, however, saw it differently. Fresh paint and rebuilt engine aside, it would only take one storm, one funky wave, one broken mast stay and we, knuckleheads and landlubbers would be on a sixty-foot raft without a prayer. It's amazing what you can ignore at 21. We would leave Boston Harbor alright, but we were going to die out there and our regrets for having been that stupid would just be so much conjecture for the living left behind.

The last line on our optimist's list was, replace the rudder. We told Jim about our plan to put the *Kilu* on a small dry dock at the back of the Marina, slap a rudder on our swan and leave.

"Don't put your boat on that," he said.

"Why?"

"Your keel is forty feet long and the dry dock is thirty. The overhang, will crack your hull right at the keel box."

Jim offered to tow us to a beach where we could run the *Kilu* in and make the repair. We turned him down. The next day we dragged our baby to the back of the marina and tied her to the chain link fence that ran right along Commonwealth Avenue. When the tide fell, we bolted our new rudder to the sternpost and hopped on board. We were solid, smug, waiting for the incoming tide to float our boat. Then Mark came up from below.

"There's water in the hold," he said. "Planking probably got dry in the air," we told ourselves. It would swell up soon.

The water got higher. A bucket brigade began, not enough. A hand pump, nope. Mechanical pump, no change. Electric pump, still flooding. Our hurried activity, some might say panic, draws tourists passing by on the street. In no time, a couple dozen people are on the other side of the fence, only a few feet away.

"What's going on?"

"Is your boat sinking?"

"Why don't you pump it out?"

I dropped two Darvon, clambered into the hold to keep the engine running. If water reached the carburetor, it was all over. In the meantime, someone, I never found out who, called the Boston Harbor Fire Department and the BHFD dispatched a fireboat to our narrow slip. I knew none of this until I heard a cheer from the pedestrians topside. It may have been the drugs, but that massive red boat looked as big as an aircraft carrier.

It hit reverse at the last minute, made a majestic stop, the diesel engines throbbing softly. The captain, who seemed a thousand feet in the air, looked at me, then nodded at a sailor who walked to the bow and threw a six-inch wide, hose over the side. I dove in, pulled it aboard and dragged it to the lowest point in our hull. Back on deck I gave the captain a thumbs up and seconds later, tons of dirty water began gushing through the tube.

There was one problem, however. Fireboats drop hoses over the side to pump water into those cannons on their deck. Our hose was still connected to the one at the bow, unattended and by chance, aimed right at the tourists behind the fence. When the pump went live, a hemorrhage of black, oily goo drenched the sightseers. The drama unfolded in seconds. The crowd ran into the street under a sodden cascade. A car lost control, smacked a light pole and blocked traffic. As rising water pressure sent the unmanned cannon skyward, its torrent followed the tourists across the road where they huddled at the wall of a ten-story condo. Their crisis ended when the giant spray passed overhead but the show wasn't over. A ton of muck splattered the side of the building, inundating a new crowd; the dozen families watching my boat sink from their balconies. Men, women, and children ran for their sliding doors while everything on the terraces, books to baby carriages, got soaked. The deluge didn't stop until the crew shut the cannon down.

When we, and probably some on the fireboat stopped laughing, the *Kilu* was afloat. This was a temporary condition and we knew it, so now we took Jim's advice and began motoring full speed to a beach, three miles away, on the other side of Boston Harbor.

It's almost sunset, Captain Mark is at the wheel. We are on our own power, making a wake in clean air under a perfect, blue sky. Our rudder's working, our tall, raked masts roll with the swell. People on docks are waving, boats, running alongside, blast their horns and cheer. *Kilu,* an icon from another century, has come alive. In the middle of our disaster, we've become champions.

Our goal is the foot of Logan Airport. We will get away with this, we will run our boat aground at an international airfield because no one had yet heard of Yassir Arafat or Osama Bin Laden. We are crashing the gate before hopelessness got personal, scoundrel and victim, all fall down, so I didn't understand as we headed into the still waters of this welcoming bay, why the boats accompanying us pulled back. The *Kilu* goes on alone and like thousands of other people that day, we land at Logan.

We plow full speed across the sand, jump off in triumph and wave goodbye to our friends in the harbor. Jet planes are landing a half mile away, yet we attract no attention. We light a fire, cook hot dogs and trade hilarious versions of the day's events before falling into our oddly tilted bunks with the boat resting on its side. Overnight, the remaining water leaked out of the hull leaving a dark trail in the sand from where, as Jim had promised, we'd cracked her back. We also saw why our friends had turned away at the bay's entrance; it was littered with boulders that somehow, at high tide, we'd passed without hitting. The morning also brought a man with a shotgun. This guy's job was to shoot birds so they wouldn't nest near the runway, be sucked into jet engines, crash the plane, kill all aboard. We shared our story and were told to get to the administration building and ask for clearance.

An hour later, with no interrogation, no background check, no questions asked, we got permission to drive in and out of the airport, cross its runways, promise not to get hit by jets landing or taking off, and generally be responsible for our own safety. We were pretty good about it though one afternoon, waiting for a 707 to make liftoff, I crossed too early and almost blew away the Pontiac's convertible top. We lived like gypsies, which wasn't a big change from life at the marina, so it didn't seem crazier than anything else until a reporter showed up from *The Boston Globe*. The next morning, the *Kilu* was on page six with a photo of Ian Jarvis in front of his beached whale, pretending to be in charge. I must admit, I liked the attention.

We still had a boat to fix. I tunneled under the hull and eventually screwed a copper patch over the crack. A few days later, with full moon tides higher than normal, the rocks plotted, we re-launched, anchored in the harbor and ran pumps every six hours to see if the leak was under control. If things were good in the morning, we'd leave for the

Caribbean in a week. At sunrise, Kilu was still afloat, so we headed back to the marina.

I thought we were getting the hang of it, but our return was somewhat blemished when Captain Mark hit reverse too late and the *Kilu* ran right into Lewis Wharf. Well, not into it, our bowsprit simply ran up over the top of the dock, lifting the front of our boat out of the water. It looked like a tug would be towing us off if the bowsprit didn't tear away first but a minute later, the *Kilu* slid gracefully back in the water on its own, like a crocodile who'd missed a kill.

Our pride was damaged and worse, ramming the dock blew away any remaining support at the Marina. A group came over. They gave us one week. "Okay, okay. We were leaving anyway." We started buying supplies, coastal maps, and in a moment of lucidity, a flare gun.

A few nights later, a guy comes into the harbor on his thirty-five-foot sloop, asks if he can tie up on the *Kilu* until a berth opens next day. He leaves for his condo. All is well until around midnight, when a rare, northeast squall blows in. It only took minutes. The winds got fierce, five-foot waves were suddenly battering our two boats, moored to my one set of old ropes. The line snapped and the *Kilu*, with a very expensive yacht attached, began drifting backwards toward Jim's steel trawler. My little engine was no match for the wind and the weight of both boats. Foot by foot—all in slow motion to me—we drew closer and closer, until the Trawler's bow crashed down on our stern. One blow was all it took; tons of water began cascading in.

I raced for the galley, grabbed my bag and made it to the deck. The bow was already lifting out of the water. Mark, who'd dropped acid several hours before, saw the hand of God at work but wasn't too overwhelmed to save the sloop. He found our axe, chopped the remaining lines and we jumped on the yacht and motored into the bay. Thirty minutes later, the squall had passed but the poor *Kilu* was on the ocean floor, her raked masts sticking out of the water like two fingers pointing at the sky. To the paying customers though, it looked like a giant, "Fuck you." They told us to get professional divers and have the sticks cut down.

"No problem," said Dumb and Dumber. "We'll meet here tomorrow and make arrangements."

The next night, Mark was again at Logan, this time boarding a plane for Beirut. I snuck back to the wharf, took my welding torches, the only thing saved from the *Kilu* and in the morning, began hitchhiking across America to see if Jane Lancaster still loved me in San Francisco.

# 3
# NICE JEWISH BOY FROM NEW JERSEY

The night I was born, my Dad made a bet with the counterman at Rutt's Hut. A girl, and Dad would buy the guy a beer. A boy, my father would get a free hot dog. He won two: one dog for me, one for twin brother Malcolm, unpredicted, unseen, soon to be unloved. Mal had a receding jaw, a look less promising. Our mother largely ignored him; an artless incision that broke my brother's heart and seared him with hair trigger rage.

In our family album is a wrinkled, black and white photo. We are five years old, a lakefront beach in Maine. Malcom's hanging onto Mom, anguished, bawling, begging for attention. She keeps her hands to herself, stays ready for the camera. I sit behind them, clear eyed, stonewall neutrality.

On a winter trip to S. Klein's department store in NYC, Mal throws himself on the floor, screaming without hope over something my mother said he couldn't have. A crowd gathers, he won't stop crying. I drift away, ashamed, can't be a part of this. Their relationship played out time and again. Seeing it transfused my heart with fear; my mother withholding love, and later, the power of girls, and then women, to do the same. *Keep your feelings to yourself. Don't say anything someone can use to hurt you.* My heart was hermetically sealed. I carried it way too long.

Mom told us we'd be a matched pair for life. Dad said we didn't play much with toys as babies, we preferred to play with each other, that we spoke late because we spoke our own language. As toddlers, I remember us dragging a kitchen chair to the fridge, reaching the door handle to open it to get more food. Sixth grade was a fork in the river; we are in separate classes, but judgment is still a juggernaut. "I like you, Ian, but Malcolm, he's . . ." I stop defending him, keep my place in the social order. I see now, how hard that must have been for him, cut off from my modest success, the friends I had. Our lives overlapped, but we lived in different orbits.

On a September night, twelve years old, we make a last stand together. Mal and I are in the back of a downtown bus. Jack Lapacca and two slicks walk on, their joy at seeing us palpable. Jack was our seventh-grade oligarch, leather jacket, hoodlum hair, he could land anywhere. His posse had already made soft passes: a word, a look, a bump in the hall. They sashay our way, sit, and stare us down. Minutes later, the stop at Van Houten, we fast-walk the street, followed by the bullshit menace. In front of our house, Jack gets in my face.

"Let's beat the shit outta the Jarvis twins!" He crows.

I'm shaking, no fight in me, want to run away, then out of nowhere, a voice in my head says, "Throw the first punch, Ian, you've got nothing to lose". I do it. A real street fight. I'm in an adrenalin envelope, don't feel the blows. They break away, Malcolm runs to the house, comes out seconds later slashing the air with a kitchen knife.

"I'm gonna kill 'em!" he screams. "Where are they, I'm gonna kill 'em!"

Dad is right behind, takes the knife, shepherds Mal home, bawling with frustration. In the morning, I have a black eye, think it's awful, the last thing I want in public. My father could step in, tell me he's proud, turn this into a badge of honor. He gives me nothing. At school, Lapacca walks up, smiling, stares at me for a second, leaves with a light tap on my shoulder. I'm anointed, the kids who see it crowd in to hear the story.

My mother was a creative, suffocated by her time and place. All that remained was a bitter goal; teach her children the world was out to get them. She threatened lawsuits, instilled paranoia, created a world of drama. My brother and sister followed her, a lifetime of distrust. When she handed me a tuna sandwich, I'd go to school knowing no matter what she said, no one was gonna steal it. I was just as certain Aunt Rose hadn't embezzled my Father's inheritance, or that Mom's last-minute intervention at Columbia was the only reason Dad got his doctorate.

My father's crime was absence, as force, as fun, as friend, as help, as inspiration. He'd seen the 1929 Depression take from his immigrant family everything they earned, and his sense of panic never abandoned him. He was Director of Music for the city's schools, guaranteed employment, but he wouldn't buy a house, wasn't getting buried like his father, if the market crashed again.

When my parents argued, Dad's exit strategy was to swallow his bile, drop into self-pity, or escape to the attic; his monk's cell where he wrote his doctoral thesis. I see the black, Remington typewriter, sitting on his desk like a crouching spider. I hear the percussive, syncopated clack of its fine-cut steel stems punching through the inked cloth ribbon to post sentence after sentence on the page. A low hum of electricity courses through the space heater at his feet, its glowing, copper shell throwing a tight tunnel of orange warmth over him as he pecks away, fingertips blue from changing the carbon paper behind every page he wrote.

With a Columbia PhD, he became "*Doctor* Maxwell Jarvis,"

and if you forgot, he'd remind you. He directed a regional orchestra, led Passaic's glee club, taught piano in our living room and gave his intelligence, patience, and deep love of music to students of all kinds. But when it came time to fire up *my* creativity, Dad handed me a French horn; fifteen feet of brass tubing with the musical presence of a substitute teacher.

"You could get a scholarship to college," he said. "They're always looking for horn players."

Really? A maybe music scholarship is why I ended up goose-stepping across the football field at halftime in a royal blue tunic with gold buttons and red stripes, under a white plumed, Shako hat? The fucking marching band? Your son was meant to leave that field bloody and bruised, steel cleats scraping the locker room floor in victory or defeat. I wanted to bind my wounds among men, snatch forty-yard passes while the enemy tried to crush me. I had the hands and speed to earn a PHS football jacket. I was sixteen, nothing mattered more.

I grew up in the gold-plated mysticism of America's Second World War; saw John Wayne, shot in the back by a dirty Jap on Mount Suribachi in, *Sands of Iwo Jima*, watched Audie Murphy singlehandedly stop a Nazi advance at the Rhine in, *To Hell and Back*, Richard Conte, blinded by a grenade in *Guadalcanal*, furiously firing his water-cooled machine gun while the camera closed in on his scared, sightless eyes and the music swelled and you knew he was going to die and he knew it too, but that was the sacrifice you made for your country. I bought it, would join the army, get a gun, go to war, never die.

I was eight when my grandfather came to stay. No one told us he had cancer. One night, my brother and I were herded into our bedroom. Tension out there, huddled conversation, strangers coming and going. When a rolling sound bumped down our narrow hall, I put one eye to the tiny keyhole, saw a gurney trundle by, white shirted arms holding a sheet over his body. No one talked about it after that. He just wasn't there.

I started phoning my parents, checking their plans, waiting at the window, imagining how many ways I might lose them. When I refused an overnight school trip, it got their attention. We sat at the red Formica, dinette table in a little alcove next to the kitchen.

"What'll happen to us," I asked in tears, "If you die . . . !" I got adult smiles, platitudes in return. I was still circling the drain, nauseated all winter.

A sunny, early spring afternoon, pacing the sidewalk, waiting for Mom to come home. I stepped out of a cold wind to a protected corner on our wood porch. The green paint, peeling with age, was warm, the sun's heat on my face, hypnotic. I closed my eyes, was half asleep when a message came in from somewhere in the universe. "Let go of the fear." The voice whispered. "Let your heart heal." I was too young to truly understand those words, but young enough to feel them. I lay still, a state of grace, while my belly unclenched, a purple light filled my eyes. In those extraordinary moments the chasm closed, the insatiable wolf disappeared. I walked to the schoolyard to play with friends, never looked back.

At sixteen I was living the teenage split; the difference between what you show your parents and what you really are. My high school pals, all of us underage, were taking family cars for joy rides, taking them from strangers too, no thought about accidents, jail time, or death. I drag raced my Father's Chevy on Jefferson Boulevard, hit 100 on Route 46 in a 'borrowed' Grand Prix, stole a 356 Porsche off a parking lot to blast past Passaic High.

One night, cool hand in a 1957 Thunderbird, a police car lit us up. "Park it back there, in the bus stop," the cop said, "and shut it off." I had skills, but made a show of fumbling for reverse, then ran the T-Bird up over the curb.

Stevie, sitting next to me, hissed, "For fuck's sake, Ian!"

The cop stepped out to manage my ineptitude. "I'm sorry, sir," I said. "Don't know how to park yet, won't have my permit for another month. Steve here, his father's out of town, a dumb move, I know."

He poked his head in, sniffed the air. I wasn't drunk, clearly hadn't done much of this. I think he was pissed off too, with the guys who'd ratted us out just to fuck me over. He and his partner conferred, checked the registration.

"Plates match up," he said. "I can book you on felony auto and no license. Car theft won't stick, but it'll sure screw with your life."

I stare at him. All innocence . . .

"Okay, hotshot. Your friend stays here. You got twenty minutes. Bring me someone with a license, I'll forget this happened."

The party where I'd carried those car keys around like a gold medal, was two blocks away. I ran back, found a legit driver, got the "Don't ever let me catch you again", lecture and not believing our luck, piled into the T-Bird and brought it home. I was sure the cop would backdoor my Dad, so my strategy, laughably inadequate, was to stay home after school and all weekend, take every phone call. The guy kept his word though. My parents never knew how close they came to walking their burgeoning bad boy into a juvie court appearance and a dishonorable mention in the *Passaic Herald Tribune*.

# 4
# LIGHTS ON – LOSING IT IN PROVINCETOWN

Passaic's, Third Ward Park; acres of scalloped ground, leafy shade trees, picnic tables, and meandering paths. Stately homes, built with textile manufacturing money at the turn of the century, lined the streets around it. Some were wood, others in stone; elegant, perfectly painted with enormous windows and rolling lawns, their Cadillacs and Lincolns parked out front.

A large, kidney shaped pond at the park's center was stocked every spring with sunnies and bluegills. I was eight years old the first time I went fishing. I found a spot near the falls and pinched a nightcrawler from the box. It squirmed in my fingers. I squeezed it hard and put the hook through the fattest part. The worm erupted with amazing strength, frenzied contractions. It escaped my hand and fell to the ground, writhing in pain around its gooey wound. I was stunned by my cruelty, I ran home to Mom, shaken, crying with remorse.

A few years later I would try again, the ocean this time at Atlantic City's shoreline. Our summers were spent there because Mom believed polio, destroyer of lungs and bodies, didn't threaten her children in the fresh, ocean air, so every June, the family drove south in Dad's black Studebaker, a car who's rocket ship styling was as confident as all America.

Malcolm and I would hunch up at the rear window squealing with excitement at every extravagant, new car.

"Pontiac Chieftain" . . . "Olds Rocket 88!" "Chrysler 300!"

"I saw it first!"

"You did not!"

"Did so!"

"Dad, are we there yet?"

Hours later, across a miles-wide, alluvial plain, Atlantic City's indelible silhouette appeared, spiked by lavish hotels like The Chelsea, The Ritz, and Chalfont Haddon Hall. The Convention Center's big, black, convex roofline stood among them like the fuselage of a giant, misplaced, airplane. The Center was home to the Ice Capades, The Miss America pageant, and countless, annual conventions for powerful unions and national men's clubs like the Elks and The Shriners. AC was their playground, the escape hatch for a dull life. They'd play poker man to man, drink til dawn, bring their wife with them or find a woman at a bar.

500,000 visitors came every year for its white sandy beaches and gentle ocean. There was horse racing, and great restaurants like The Knife and Fork. The 500 Club, mob owned, as lavish as any in New York, had showstoppers like Dean Martin and Jerry Lewis, Frank Sinatra, Sammy Davis Jr.

The boardwalk, the town's suture, ran ten miles from Starn's inlet to Margate beach, cheap commerce bellied up to it most of the way. Mal and I prowled there at night, weaving in and out of the strolling crowds, couples in cocktail dresses and suits, out for dinner or a ride in the rattan prams pushed by black men who lived in the ghetto west of Atlantic Avenue. We'd cut away to explore Steel Pier, Million Dollar Pier, the Diving Bell, the Diving Horse. We played pinball games and take ferris wheel rides, surrounded by the sweet smell of cotton candy and buttered popcorn.

We saved our allowance to buy thick, saltwater taffy with exotic, tingling flavors like peppermint and banana. In front of the Planters Peanuts store, a man in a peanut, costume, smiling behind a monocle and swinging his cane, cajoled families to come inside. AC's decay, its post war death by superhighways and jet planes, that was invisible to us. All we saw were endless summers, adventure and freedom, no end in sight.

My parents rented down market, north end of town, at the Yuckman's Victorian house, where a dozen Jewish families shared kitchen and bath. First morning there, we bolted breakfast and ran to the beach, Mom yelling, "Don't go swimming for a half hour or you'll get cramps!"

We'd throw ourselves in the cold surf, yelling like tribesmen. That night, Mom would coat our sunburns with pink, Calamine lotion, but by July we were deep tanned, our brown hair, blond from the sun and salt water. When it rained, we stayed on our wide, front porch playing Monopoly or chess, but any other day, we were early to the water, giddy, bobbing on outlawed inner tubes until the muscled, handsome lifeguards showed up to whistle us in. We'd have given anything to be them, sit in their towers, girls circling, innocent, impressed, begging for attention.

I got deep into fishing; flounder, weakies, stripers and bluefish. I took a paper route at home to pay for the best equipment. From June to September, I stood waist high in Atlantic City's surf or on seaweed slippery jetties, their rocks, jumbled like broken glass. I'd sweep the ocean for clues; a tiny disturbance, baitfish jumping, a tern diving, a swirl, anything that marked the cycle of life below the surface. I loved the hunt, the patience it took, the sudden hit, all my senses in play to bring food home for my family.

Alone one night, fishing at the tip of the Vermont Avenue jetty, a guy showed up, real conversationalist, asked what I was fishing for, where I was from, Then he shifted to girls, and shifted again to how they looked, naked. He knew what he was doing, knew what would happen to a boy my age. I don't remember how, but he got my dick out and began pulling on it, the sensation, a dizzy override on confusion or fear. I was okay, I really was, right until he leaned in and whispered, "You have a big one." That's when I saw his bright eyes, his eager mouth. I panicked, and though it wasn't true, I shouted, "There's people on the boardwalk!"

In an instant, my professor of pleasure was gone. I pulled up my pants, made a few casts, feeling shocked, strange, a little depressed even, but there was only one thought on my mind. *What would've happened if he hadn't stopped?* Thirty minutes later I was on the green, corduroy sofa bed, my twin brother, dead asleep next to me because that's how you sleep at thirteen. I picked up where my explorer left off and it felt good, no confusion this time. What I'd walked away from on that jetty became clear, palpable, an attack, a bullet, a jet plane, a phantom energy whipping from my belly to my feet, dancing on my head, pressing into my heart. Something was coming, I was sure of that, I just didn't know what. Then, without warning, every muscle in my body coiled up, locked my chest, clamped my lungs and pumped out my swollen, aching, finally released cock, a hot, sticky spray that landed everywhere, my face, my hands, my legs, the bed. I didn't move, didn't exhale, gripped my cock to keep the feeling as it ebbed away. I fell into a warm, buttery sleep. I'd cracked the code. An amazing experience was mine on demand, and I, I, I, Ian Jarvis, was transformed.

Back home in September, sister Freya at college, I got my own room and put a lock on the door. Among many fantasies was the day I'd left grammar school late, walked out the front doors just as my third grade teacher, the blond haired, Miss Grabowski, fell face first, down the steps. Her skirt flew up and I saw her stockings, garter belts and underwear; the same exotics I'd picked through in my mother's dresser when she was out. Miss Grabowski wasn't hurt, she stood up quickly, more embarrassed than I was, but seeing her like that, the mystery under her skirt, thrilled me again and again. I never thought about the reams of yellow, stained newspaper Mom took out of my wastebasket every week. She didn't say a word, but I imagine both my parents had a good laugh about it.

A year later, best friend, Joey, whose father sold plumbing by day and porn films at night, stole a 16 mm reel from his dad's basement cache. We didn't know anything about sex; Jon Lenz had bragging rights for feeling up his girlfriend. My parents were out of town that weekend, so we invited Michael, Jon, Barry, and Steve, six of us, a band of brothers, to come over and see what happens, what the words mean, what this whole dark, unspoken, magical business looks like.

We take Mom's Chinese prints off the living room wall, drag the red sofa aside and thread the glossy film into our clickety-clack, Bell and Howell projector and wait, oh my God, so excited for our movie to begin. It's grainy, silent, black and white, but we don't care, we are on a voyage of discovery. Our hero, a middle aged "dentist" wears a fake beard, a black eye patch and a white lab coat. His patient sashays in, sexy, blond, voluptuous, no disguise about that. The two of them make small talk. Our overweight guy – he could have had two heads for all we cared – escorts his patient to the dental chair, puts her in full recline. He drapes a handkerchief over her mouth, pours liquid on it, chloroform see, so she'll sleep. Our angel closes her eyes. He looks her over – did he really twirl his mustache? – then circles the chair and drops his pants.

The camera closes in, shows us what it looks like, the crease between her thighs, the penetration, how this thing works. Our girl, despite being sedated, raises her legs and gets into it and so do we, edging closer to the screen with guileless, teenage hard-ons. When our fifteen-minute blockbuster ends, we hit my father's liquor cabinet for a bottle of vodka and run it again, and again, and after a dozen showings we do the only thing left, a circle jerk on Mom's white carpet, no judgement, no cares, pure joy. We've seen what we can't have, not with stay-at-home mothers and tight girdles and strict morals, but we know a thing or two now, we are close, we are almost men.

Everything was working for America then, anything was possible. We were safe, in a strong economy, a system we believed. There were no riots, marches or wars, and without crises or national tension, our horizons got wide and our choices too. I was still inside my generation's thin optic; college, marriage, kids, but the ground was opening, it wouldn't take much to shake me out.

At sixteen, I'm looking forward to another summer in Atlantic City followed by senior year at PHS. My friends at the shore, Mickey, Elaine and Dave – we fish together – are older, already on mission at Temple University, tracking as doctors and lawyers. They get summer work with the Safeway supermarket on Pacific Avenue, big place, a dozen check-out lines. A slot opens. I lie about my age, excited to have a real job. The manager, bad decision, makes me a cashier. There were no electronic chips to read prices and do the math, not then, so cashiers figured out correct change by themselves. It was simple stuff, add and subtract, only math wasn't in my toolbox. All I remember about fourth grade is Mom and I, meeting for months after school at our blond wood, dining room table. She'd hold up big, brightly colored, flash cards, answers on the back, mindnumbing repetition until I memorized the multiplication table so I would not get left a grade behind. That was good enough for school, but I'm on my own at Safeway. Management counts the cash trays every day. Mine is always short, a drumbeat that gets me fired within a month.

My sister, Freya, waitress at a Howard Johnson's restaurant in Massachusetts, puts me up for a position and just like that I'm gonna to be a busboy in some place called, Provincetown on Cape Cod. All I knew about the Cape was that its location, twenty miles off the coast, made it a nexus for the holy grail of surf fishing; schools of thirty- and forty-pound striped bass in numbers that were unimaginable in New Jersey. I was excited, packed my fishing gear and got ready to leave.

I didn't know Provincetown was the first layover for America's founding fathers; the radical, Calvinist zealots who claimed the Church of England was a fornicating house of sin. They weren't wrong, but all they got for it were orders to leave. The Pilgrims, as they were called, one hundred of them, sailed for the New World on a boat called The Mayflower but it was a rough Atlantic crossing, the winter of 1620, so they dropped anchor in P-town's protected harbor for a few months of R&R before sailing on to Plymouth to do God's work; fuck the natives over, then claim the entire continent for themselves.

Three hundred years later, Provincetown was still a refuge for social outcasts. The year-round population, a few thousand, mostly Portuguese fishermen and their families, lived in tidy, wood houses with tiny front yards enclosed by picket fences. The streets were narrow, cobbled, not a traffic light in site. Nights were cooled by ocean breezes, and everything, and everyone, was in walking distance. Provincetown, at the very tip of the Cape, had a magical attraction. Just getting there, the drive itself, felt like you'd reached the end of a rainbow. The town was swollen every summer with tens of thousands of tourists. Serving them was a crowd of volunteers who came to dream, drug, fuck and hustle; musicians, magicians, beatnik tribes, and road warriors.

The biggest crowd though, was gay. In America, persecuting

"homos" was a civic duty, right up there with voting and the Fourth of July. Payback for getting caught with their pants down ran from beatings and jail time to social and economic dismemberment. Not in P-town. There were occasional busts for behavior unbecoming, but the collars wound up in front of a local judge who ignored America's moral compass; he knew how much money the gay crowd left behind.

Freya was in Provincetown to explore her sexuality, too. She hadn't dropped that intel on Mom and Dad, so they blessed my departure and a week later I traded cow-town Atlantic City, for the wildest ten square miles on the East coast. At sixteen, I was a unicorn there; my generation wasn't in the mix yet. Baby Boomers weren't on the radar, we hadn't done anything, hadn't gotten high, invented bellbottoms, taken acid, burned our draft cards, marched on Washington. My generation was just getting started when I showed up at Freya's sparsely furnished, three bed rental to doss down with her girlfriends from McGill University. I slept on the sofa listening to Joan Baez warble, "House of The Rising Sun." The other girls liked me, would throw an omelet together in the morning, but Sis wasn't happy walking her one-night stands past baby brother, so we agreed not to tell our parents and I went out to find my own place.

I met Murray Green, owner of a tchotchke store on the main drag, Commercial Street. Murray sold T-shirts, beachwear, and rubber rafts under a large, faded, Half Off Sale, banner. Behind his shop was the original, Provincetown Theater. Above it, he had a rooming house for artists and drifters, a warren of bare walls, bowed floors, and swayback beds. Afternoons, I'd sit at my window, watch the crowds spill over the sidewalks, shopping for T-shirts, lobster rolls, and crap art.

My roommate was Dick Pettengill, late twenties, handsome, strong jawed, an easy laugh. He rolled with the punches, wintered in Florida working construction, had no plans other than to do exactly what he wanted. Next to us, in a studio with a wall of windows facing the bay, was Bill Sullivan, artist and lover of men, Dave Ridley lived across the hall. He owned a Triumph motorcycle, took me to work one day on the scenic route via Race Point. It was my first ride; thirty minutes like a fighter pilot, exhilarated, leaning into turns, accelerating down the straights, the noise, the wind, the danger. I stepped off that bike inside a halo of Brando's swaggering masculinity.

A week after starting at the Howard Johnson's restaurant, aka, Ho Jo's, I had the brilliant idea that rather than get up each time a booth emptied, it would be far more efficient to wait until half a dozen tables were dirty. I'd leave food on the floor, spilt milk, greasy napkins, spaces no one could sit in, until I felt the time was right to clean. It was a real insult to the staff and owners and I'll never know why I wasn't fired or at least talked to for an attitude adjustment. I would not have put up with me!

One night I woke to Dick, rapping his knuckles on my head. He was fucking a pretty girl with short, black hair and bless his heart he wanted me to see, first time ever, a naked woman. I was dazzled by her flesh, her pert breasts rolling like Jello as she rocked back and forth, moaning with pleasure. I went on full alert, a neutral observer, cataloging the moves, sponging up the craft, taking note of Dick's hands on her hips, guiding their rhythm, the positions, placement, whispered words. In the morning, they were gone, but Pettengill's friend had left me a note "Nice seeing you last night, Ian." She signed it, "Love Erin", with a cheeky little heart. Provincetown wasn't a fishing expedition anymore. I'd crash landed in a growing-up factory. I might get laid here.

Everyone was fucking, everyone but me. Girls would flirt, get bright eyed, but when they found out how old I was, they'd sigh, kiss my cheek and leave. Even Estelle, a woman that lived at the back of our boarding house, who would sweep me into her room and sleep with me, never gave it up; she just liked spooning. Everyone figured we were having sex, and I was coy about my answers, assumptions were made, but I was still waiting for a real consecration.

I was untethered, no rules, no oversight, no one to report to. After work, I often went with the staff to jazz clubs or parties. Some days, I motored out to sea with three locals, tough guys in a small boat, scuba diving for lobsters. There were two rules, find my divers when they surfaced - which could get freaky when the wind was high - and cut loose every bag if I saw a Coast Guard boat speeding my way. There were bound to be pregnant females in our sacks, the fine was a dollar per egg and a pregnant lobster had thousands.

Pettengill took me to a party at Norman Mailer's one night. Mailer was literature's lion, and his writing, especially The *Naked and The Dead*, got my attention; muscular, edgy, never seen that before. He was known to drink, take on anybody he didn't like, got himself arrested once for DWI and insulting the P-town cops. He turned down a plea deal, defended himself, convinced a jury of his peers to let him off. When he seriously wounded his sixth wife with a kitchen knife, he beat that rap, too. This time though, payback was three months in Bellevue. A lot of people believed they should have kept him there, but Mailer was gifted and brave, and he got away with everything.

I was invited to gay parties. They knew I was underage, flirted constantly, but like the women in town, never made a real move. I liked the attention, was excited to be noticed. At one of those parties, I met Walter Chrysler Jr, a Detroit prince, cast out from the automotive kingdom for his dubious sexuality. Money was Walt's leverage but his oxygen was self-aggrandizement. Walter Senior had built the world famous, art deco, Chrysler Building in Manhattan. Junior wanted a monument to himself; a Museum in Provincetown for the huge, international, art collection he'd been acquiring since the 1930s

Walter was so cheap he'd sit outside his temporary quarters on

Commercial Street to collect the entry fees himself. He was imperious, demanding, and eventually he wore out his welcome. The P-Town deal fell apart so he left for Norfolk, Virginia. They didn't like his sexual preferences, but they wanted his money and soon, Norfolk had the Chrysler Museum of Art, a proud addition to the city's growing stature, until *Life Magazine* published an article remarking that half the paintings on those hallowed halls were fakes.

*Life* said that Walter knew it too, so a lot of skinny canvasses came down overnight. Today, the museum website graciously says, "Walter made some good trades and some, not-so-good trades." They were all good trades to Jimmy LePere, the New York art dealer who brokered many of them, and fifteen years after the debacle, I was, by chance, renting a studio in Jimmy's Lower East Side townhouse when fate circled me back to Chrysler. Jimmy's brownstone, a splash of elegance on the corner of 2nd Avenue and 3rd Street, was a few hundred feet from the largest men's shelter in NYC. LePere's sidewalk became an oasis for men discharged from the shelter every morning. They'd drop their bags at Jimmy's cast iron railings, pool their change for a gallon of Thunderbird wine from the bulletproof liquor store across the street, then hang out on our corner till the shelter re-opened. Their clubhouse, just outside my window, was a real democracy, a subculture whose currency was cigarettes, regrets, and percussive insults about space and possessions. Furious, fluid, sometimes violent, they drove Jimmy nuts. Every few days he'd scatter the crowd with a baseball bat, but once the threat was gone, they'd drift back like a flock of sidewalk pigeons.

When Chrysler and I met at Jimmy's, I didn't tell him about P-Town, but one day Sir Walter invited me to lunch at Le Cote Basque. *What the fuck's on his mind?* After The Chef's Tasting Menu and two bottles of Laffite Rothschild, Walt suggested I become LePere's lover! The Chrysler Foundation, he promised, would, "Make it worth my while." All I knew, was Jimmy liked rough trade and weird guys, and

Walter's promised rewards, weren't anywhere near enough to put me on the receiving end of my landlord's funky predilections. (Jimmy would die of AIDS a few years later, claiming it was only brain cancer.)

A few weeks after declining Walt's kind offer, I was kicked out of my $175/month, ground floor studio filled with great African art, a gigantic glass chandelier, and a working fireplace. I also left behind, and this really hurt, access to the third-floor sex club, run by one of Jimmy's friends, a vague, British art dealer named Jan Milner, a guy so rich or pretending to be, that his blue sport coat's solid gold buttons had to be removed before every dry cleaning.

The day Milner launched his laboratory, I found a woman in a white cowboy hat, white bra, and stockings, near my door. She checked me out with the clear-eyed assessment of a surgeon. It was her outfit though, that got my attention. She was dressed like Allie, the sweet, older woman in Provincetown who in my sixteenth year, blessed me with manhood.

The wildcats I hung out with in P-town ignored my age. If I walked into the Atlantic House with them, there was a seat at the bar for anything non-alcoholic. One night, end of summer, I was there with Eddie Sears, a remarkable jazz pianist. Eddie drifted over to a table of friends. I stayed at the bar; I liked seeing everything from that vantage point and watching the Bartender work the room. He rang a small, ship's bell every time he got a tip. Handsome guy, the first man I'd ever seen with an earring. A tall woman, two seats away, long blond hair and jeans, heard me order orange juice.

"Not drinking?" she said.

"Under twenty-one, I'm with those guys."

Allie smiled, and came over. "How old *are* you?"

" ... Sixteen."

"How did you get to P-town? No one's here that young."

I figured she was in her thirties, told her the story.

"Come to my place," she said. "It's too expensive to keep drinking at the bar."

In the car, she looked me over, her eyes bright with the pleasure of my innocence. She asked about high school, what I thought of my hometown, pretty much a one-way conversation, though she did say she was a dancer, up from the city for a month. At her apartment, she opened a bottle of wine. I didn't drink, so I was soon stoned. When I apologized, she said, "That's okay Ian," and slid my middle finger in her mouth. " . . . that feels good . . . " I murmured. She put my hand on her breast, leaned in and whispered. "You're a virgin, aren't you?" I nodded.

"Wait here," she said. A few minutes later, Allie returned in white stockings, white bra, and panties. She walked over, unzipped me, pulled my cock out and said, "Very nice, Ian. You deserve a special night. Take your pants off, sweetheart." Allie slid herself over me, began whispering stuff in my ear. I came in minutes of course, but she knew that would happen. We'd do it again later that night, and she would show me what she wanted, show me a lot - my first time making love. I left in the morning, convinced I'd return to Provincetown for the rest of my life.

# 5
# GEORGETOWN UNIVERSITY

A, "C" average in high school meant my college prospects fell somewhere between Boston U and Rutgers. I only applied to Georgetown because the Senior Advisor said, "Don't waste your time, you'll never get in." GU sent an alumnus for an interview. After we spoke, he said, "You should think about a business administration degree," I thought, *Business? Never going to be one of thoes guys.*

    GU's acceptance letter arrived a month later. I stepped right up, never visited the campus, though I did find some pics which looked great; classic, Harvard-Princeton-style, hundred year old stone buildings, covered in ivy, manicured lawns, trees, wide pathways for students and staff, exactly what I thought I wanted. I didn't know the school was unimaginative, unconscious, a walled-in community for a dying breed. I didn't even know it wasn't co-ed!

    For freshman orientation week, I could think of nothing more embarrassing than showing up with mom and dad, so I took a train to Washington D.C. and became pretty much the only student without their bright-eyed parents, floating around campus like a flock of penguins, introducing themselves and their kids to everyone they met. My next tremor of doubt was at the entrance to my dorm; a huge floating banner that said, **Welcome, Gentlemen of Georgetown**. Things got worse. GU's concession to the twentieth century was abolishing mandatory chapel the year I got there but freshmen were still expected to self-infantilize by wearing straw, boater hats and reporting to the dorm manager by 9:00 PM, lights out at 11:00. This P-Town veteran was appalled. I wouldn't wear their stupid hat, cut my long hair, or get coffee for upperclassmen. Screw the Pope, end of story.

At Jesuit schools the chancellor was a priest, others taught courses. A few roamed our halls to visit the prettier boys, which meant I got a fly-by most nights, from an elderly servant of God, his eyes alight, his voice dappled with lust. I was blue eyed, black haired and olive skinned, and he didn't know, a race apart, one of fifteen Jews in a class of 1,400. We weren't the only underserved population on campus. D.C. was more than 50 percent black, but my Georgetown University had less than six on its picture-perfect campus and none, on its all-white, basketball team.

My classmates, not very Christian about apostacy, were in my face, some promising I'd eat my teeth if I didn't straighten out, get a haircut, and fly right. But all resistance ended the October afternoon Jacqueline Hunter, high school senior, red haired, long legged, fearless, and privileged, stood at the entrance to my Georgetown University dorm, a place where no women were allowed unless they were black, underpaid, and making our beds.

Jacquiline, intent on bagging her virginity and sure I was the man to do it, decided not to wait in the courtyard for some nameless freshman to deliver her invitation. She would do it herself. I was in my top floor room, cramming for an exam when I heard a buzzing sound downstairs like a swarm of angry bees. It got louder, closer, and turned shrill and undulating. I had no idea my new girlfriend, the first co-ed in men's dorm history to grace its marble stairs, was gathering dozens of freshmen on every floor she passed; a mob, delirious over her audacity.

The guys in my hall heard it too and began drifting to the center stairwell to see what was going on. About a dozen of us were there when Jacquiline Hunter, a girl I was never going to forget anyway, burst through the doors, wrapped a hand around my neck, French kissed me in front of a hundred Georgetown University freshmen and whipped away all confusion, any doubt that the skinny kid in the corner room, insecure, uncertain, at sea like any seventeen-year-old, was despite all that, the first man in the community.

A month later, I became starting goalie for GU's freshman soccer team. I'd never played the game, but the coach saw me hanging out with a few guys, kicking the ball all the way to midfield. Our first match was at the University of Maryland. In the second half, a penalty kick, awarded to the other side, had me facing a guy who eventually took his skills to the NFL.

If our coach had explained the tactics of defending a penalty shot, I'd have picked a direction, left or right, and lunged that way just before the ball was kicked because it would've given me 50/50 chance to at least, leap in the right direction. I was a soccer dummy however, so I just stood my ground, thinking I'd jump once I saw where it was going. My opponent, believing I would lunge one way or another, hit the ball right down the middle where he was sure I wouldn't be. A speed of light, banana kick was suddenly coming right at my head and I, in a state of primeval self-defense, threw my hands up just in time to parry the ball over the goalpost. My entire team charged across the field to celebrate the brilliant play. That move gave me a new life; drinking beer til curfew with the jocks, and invitations to their parties at fraternity houses off campus. I was cruising the road to acceptance.

In November, I heard the Glee Club had booked a tour to Puerto Rico over the Christmas vacation, so I joined up. The night before our flight, we were all to meet in NYC. After dinner we'd review rules and regulations, then go to bed, two gentlemen of Georgetown, to a room.

I skipped the pow wow, snuck out to meet Eddie Sears, my jazz pianist friend from Provincetown. I didn't know Eddie was a junkie or that our night out would be a tour of NYC's heaviest neighborhoods; lower East Side, Hell's Kitchen, Upper West and finally Harlem. I sat in the car at each stop, under a heavy rain, motor running to keep warm. I watched New York's street life through the windshield; washed out images of traffic, flashing neon signs, people hunched over trying to get home. When he finally scored, Eddie told me he'd been fighting with his wife, Carole, asked if he could sleep in my room. I didn't think much about it, so off we went to a floor full of GU frosh. Fortunately, it was late and everyone, including my roommate, was asleep.

Eddie shot up in the bathroom and came to bed. I was non-judgmental about his habits until he put a hand over my leg and began rubbing my cock. I was stunned yet did nothing. I had to admit, it felt hot but if my roommate woke to a scene from the gay life, that would have been the end of my career at Georgetown.

"I can't, Eddie." I whispered, pushing him away. I remember to this day, his sigh, his full stop, disappointment, the long seconds before he got out of bed to dress, apologize, and leave. I wouldn't see him again for five years.

The next day the Glee Club landed in San Juan, officially welcomed by the Puerto Rican Alumni Association. Their idea of all-expenses paid was a naval barracks outside San Juan where forty-five teenagers in bunk beds began stealing blankets, farting, joking, and yelling from one end of the hall to the other. I got lucky. A freshman friend, Esteban Blanco – his father was a Supreme Court Justice in Puerto Rico, came over to say hello the next day, saw the chaos and took me to stay with his family in Santurce. I made all performances but no dinners, drinks, nothing. Esteban and I water skied, hit the beaches, drove out to the hills to have roast pig and beers under a canopy of palm and coconut trees. I had a great time, even got laid. The day we landed in D.C., can't blame them, they fired me.

I had fun at GU, but life there was monochrome white, privileged, a real bore. I kept up with tests and papers and classes, – a mighty, 'C' average again – but it was like I'd never left high school; a mind-numbing cycle of memorization, not a moment where serious ideas came up for air. I know it sounds naive but honestly, that's what I wanted, that's what I though college would be.

I asked the school if I could move off campus at the end of my first semester. That went nowhere, which is why most Fridays I hitchhiked two hundred miles, to Passaic. Saturday night, I'd borrow my father's Chevy, drive to Great neck, Long Island, pick up Janice, the rebellious, 16 year old Jewish girl I'd slept with in Puerto Rico. Then we'd drive to the Henry Hudson hotel in NYC, fuck for hours, and drive back to Great Neck because her mother thought her underage daughter was out with girlfriends. A few hours later, Sunday morning I'd hitchhike back to D.C. in time for curfew.

Sophomore year, I moved off campus, found an ad for a roommate in a local bar called The Rathskeller; some guy named Carl Bernstein, a cub reporter at the *Washington Star*, covering muggings, social events, and traffic accidents. Carl seduced older women, didn't clean his room or himself, and covered his rent by overcharging me for mine. We would hang out, write articles for the *National Inquirer* about spaceships landing in the D.C. suburbs, or boats lost in the Bermuda Triangle. One night, he brought in a blue labeled, 78 rpm RCA Victor record, to play the scratchy anthems of The Lincoln Brigade and explain the idealism of the 1939, Spanish Civil War. Weeks later, after he'd read the entire *Warren Report* on JFK's assassination, he howled about the whitewash, the bullshit lie it was. I deflowered his sister, had dinner with his parents, and realized years later, where his instincts came from;

the ones that let Carl Bernstein see the Watergate break-in as more insidious, more cancerous, more connected than anyone knew.

That's because Carl came to his profession with a PhD in cynicism; a perfect irony since he earned it from the FBI. The men of Quantico, doing their duty during the Red Scare in the 1950s, had subpoenaed Carl's father to testify before the House, Un-American Activities Commission. Al, a lawyer for trade unionists and communists, was asked to rat people out only he wouldn't, so the FBI trailed the Bernsteins, interviewed them, tapped their phones and interviewed them again. They took photos, followed Al's children and told their teachers about the dirty commies in their classroom.

It was hard on the family, but while stealing Carl's innocence and his childhood, the Feds gave him the anger, the drive, the "been-there-seen-that, know what this smells like," to get off his ass and follow Watergate past the American dream, the naysayers, and the national belief that we held the moral high ground. My roommate, enraged by the FBI, empowered by *The Washington Post*, and partnered with Bob Woodward, would, a few years later, win a Pulitzer Prize for the reporting that brought down our criminal, thirty-seventh President of The United States, Richard Milhouse Nixon.

It was while living with Carl that my path went through Robert F. Kennedy. I drove my Triumph motorcycle from our apartment on Dupont Circle to the Gated Community every day. There were only a few guys with bikes at Georgetown, but it was my dress code that stood out – black leather jacket and engineer's boots – a vision some girls at the Nursing School next door, couldn't take their eyes off. The boys on campus tried to ignore me when I bent over my midnight blue speedster, primed the carb, crushed the starter and brought to life with an unmuffled roar, the mystery under my control. It was the golden time, before helmets were law, so nothing got in the way of your

Ray Bans and how good you looked whether you felt that way or not, when you tapped the shift lever and slipped into traffic with a graceful, untouchable S-shaped merge.

And on a day I could have stopped at a yellow light but didn't, a day I could have stayed in bed five minutes longer but hadn't, on the day I was fated to connect with Robert Kennedy, I parked my bike at GU just as Father Richard McSorley walked past. A fifty-year-old with the face of a hawk, we began talking motorcycles. The good Father borrowed my Bonneville a few times, his black robe fluttering behind him like a wing. This guy was special; he'd been a pacifist, spent five years in a Japanese concentation camp, marched with Martin Luther King and said mass for the Kennedy family the day JFK was killed.

McSorley also led a team of nuns, tutoring Bobby's kids, who didn't give a shit about Catholic school or anything else since they were Kennedys and the Good Lord, and their good parents had bigger goals for them. One day, McSorley asked if I'd go to Hickory Hill and meet RFK and discuss a maybe job. That afternoon I curled up in the back seat of a black Cadillac limo and crossed the Potomac to a big, white, countryside mansion on a hilltop; Bobby's compound, whose only security was a few steel pipes in the ground to keep cows off the driveway. Minutes later, inside his fine home, I met Robert and Ethel, she with perfect, blond, teased hair, and he, short, muscular, intense, a killer, Boston accent.

"I understand you ride motorcycles."

"Yes."

"Look, we've got a kind of golf cart at Hyannis Port, the kids love it. It's got a BMW motorcycle engine, running lights and brakes. It's licensed to go on the road. Would you be interested in driving it down here?"

"It's open, right, no doors?"

"... Yes."

"And the brakes, they're mechanical, not hydraulic?"

"Yes, I believe so."

"Okay, what you're suggesting, it's kind of dangerous and anyway, I'll get stopped by the police every ten minutes. What if we rent a truck, I load it in and drive that down."

Kennedy stared at me, his eyes lighting up with reality, this kid's easy way out. The next day, a pocketful of cash, I was back in Bobbie's limo, this time to Dulles airport. In Boston, I booked a hotel. rented a truck in the morning and drove to Hyannis Port, where a police escort took me to the Kennedy compound. It was Rose herself who made tea and small talk. Under a bright sky and warm sun, I walked the beach where football had been played, dinners cooked, and boats raced; hallowed ground; the golden time when the Kennedy clan created its narrative, delivered a dynasty and lost it all, to two, low end assassins.

The cart they were loading on my truck had made the cover of *Life Magazine*; John Fitzgerald, himself, barreling along that beach, his huge smile, bright eyes, flowing hair and the confident promise we would all be okay even if he did break a few rules, because charm and character and knowing your history would keep America profitable and safe regardless of Castro, Khrushchev, or nuclear war.

I left the compound, disconnected the limiter on the truck and sped down I-95 to Washington. I offloaded Kennedy's new toy in Georgetown and took it on a victory lap to Hickory Hill where Bobby tossed me a pair of swimming trunks and invited me to the pool for a swim. We talked about school, his kids, my life. Kennedy's people called several times after that to do jobs for him. The kids called too. I was invited once to test a motorcycle jump they'd built. I hung out with Joseph, ten years old, while he fed live mice to a python in the basement, had a water pistol fight with Bobby Jr. in his father's bedroom. There was even talk of me coming to Hyannis Port, summer of my junior year, as ringmaster to his kids, but I was already easing out of Georgetown. I was over English Lit and Art history. I wasn't learning, hadn't found a thread of excitement. There had to be more.

In Provincetown, the most interesting people were the artists and outlaws. I wasn't sure I wanted to be one, I just wanted to be around them, find out more. I applied to Goddard College in Vermont, the other end of the educational spectrum. You were expected to follow your inspiration, become an expert in anything that turned you on. You could even design your own course, no grades, no rules, but you'd still graduate with a Bachelor of Arts. The school had good ideas when it started in the 1930's but by the time I showed up, it had lost its way. David Mamet—we acted in plays together there—called it, "Summer camp."

When Goddard accepted me, it was time to tell my parents. They were furious, my father wanted his money back! It was hard for my generation's parents. They'd worked long and hard for us, but we treated our lives like pinball games. When I told them I'd move to Mexico if they didn't buy into the change, they caved.

Now it was time to tell GU. When you quit there, you report personally to the Chancellor.

"I'm sorry you're leaving." He said.

"Why?" I asked, surprised he even knew who I was.

"You have elements of greatness," was his reply.

That ten second dialogue meant nothing at the time, except that I never forgot it. I know now, when you play back the movie of your life, those are the clips that matter.

# 6
# THE ACID TEST

In the sixties, Valium and Darvon were easing millions of rattled Americans to sleep, confident a Dexedrine pill in the morning would turn up the tempo in time to cook, clean or go to work. Our parents were taking drugs to feel normal. We took ours to feel anything *but* normal.

I joined the revolution on my twentieth birthday. I'd only been at Goddard a month, was hanging out with a dozen friends, passing joints. They seemed so relaxed and confident, I didn't know what to do. My fear of losing control had kept me straight when all around me people were getting high, but on that night, I wanted to belong, so I inhaled, and inhaled again.

Ten minutes later, nothing magical was going on. *Okay, all good, you're better than this, don't need it,* But then, out of nowhere, I chortled, even though nobody said anything funny. It happened again soon after, and then, off absolutely nothing, a head shaking laugh, a visceral shift, unexpected euphoria, a peek at the message I'd been hearing for months; that certainty was an unearned privilege, facts were fiction, time could disappear like yesterday's rain. *Fuck me. Is that possible?*

At the very moment America's presumptions were fading like

smoke from a dead fire, my generation questioned all convention, turned away from war, rolled our own and generally scared the hell out of everyone else. Millions of teenagers were about to bond over breaking the law and that was a revolution. But like all of them, ours eventually cascaded into a pecking order. School; not to be taken seriously. Sex; go down like milk. Money: dirty stuff, don't touch it. Top rung, the holy grail, was LSD, Lysergic Acid Diethylamide. Our Pied Piper, Harvard professor, Timothy Leary, got thousands of pure tabs from the Swiss by framing his fun as science, and when President Nixon declared him, "The most dangerous man in America," Leary became a prince, and trippers became aristocrats.

They told us, on LSD, the world was flat, you could see one end to the other. They said the first tab transformed physics, relationships, logic, you'd never be the same. We heard about the bad trips too, where fear became panic, became regret. Early adopters tried to fly from rooftops, walk through fire, drive with their eyes closed. Soon, middle-class kids were rolling into emergency rooms nationwide and Congress, finding an issue they could all agree on, made LSD illegal. But this is America. List any recreational drug a Class-A felony and entrepreneurs everywhere will take up the mission. Owsley Stanley, roadie for the Grateful Dead, kitchen chemist, brewed ten thousand acid tabs for an army of unwashed kids who rolled into San Francisco to make music, sleep in the park, give away their possessions and do whatever Leary told them, "Turn on. Tune in. Drop out.", he said, and we did.

My psychedelic expedition began on a cloudless September day in Westmount; a picket-fence suburb. Girlfriend, Susan Moss and I were in the grassy backyard behind her father's optometry office. We were there because Dad was out of town. He and I weren't talking, because months before, his daughter had asked for an exam, something about itchy eyes. Under the bright lights, he found a colony of crabs on her eyelashes. He dumped my bags in the street and screamed, "Take your damn sexual revolution somewhere else!"

We were stoned, it was nice, I suggested we have a spin on Dad's exam chair which I knew, was in perfect working order. Susan laughed and pulled two small squares of paper out of an envelope, a red dot on each one. She really wanted to trip with me, she said. We'd go deep, be incredible together. I fell quiet, not sure I should surrender to the beast, LSD. What would it show me? What would I show Susan? She saw my uncertain eyes, grinned, swallowed her tab and gave me a hug. "It's a perfect day," she said.

A half hour later, I was on a very solid pot high but Susan, acid veteran, her neural pathways pre-lubricated, was already tripping. She had what turned out to be a really bad idea. "Let's drive to the city for some ice cream!" she said, eyes beaming. I was closing in on Def Con Three, which may be why I couldn't find a reason *not* to bisect the Montreal metropolis for a vanilla cone. I stumbled to the car, a three speed, Gray Plymouth, and delicately merged onto Fleet Road. This would not have been insane if it wasn't my first moments on Acid and my senses weren't fried like an egg. I was consumed; splitting my focus between tamping down a hallucinating landscape and elevating the skills to deal with it; the peril of traffic lights that went off like traps, visual distortions, begging for my attention, crosstown traffic and pedestrians who from my pov, were as unpredictable as drunks.

Somehow, I got through though, and capped it with a horrendously timed left turn, crossing three lanes of angry, honking, oncoming traffic before I got into the parking lot. When I pulled up at the ice cream shop, Susan dropped into her seat, waving one hand, back and forth across her face like a windshield wiper. I was still white knuckling the steering wheel, so I shut the engine off and exhaled, long and slow, figuring it would bring down my heart rate. Unfortunately, that deft move released all constraints, delivering total lift off instead. I watched my breath, every round, white molecule of it, billow out my mouth, roll across the dashboard and cascade to the floor.

My unearned path to the unexplored universe was beginning in a concrete strip mall, on an asphalt lot, with spindly trees fronting stores selling dry cleaning and burgers. I wasn't watching a forest undulate on a verdant hillside, it was the sidewalk rippling like a belly dancer. Those brilliant, vibrating colors I was slated to see were neon signs. Pure love, acid's number one outcome, was nowhere in sight. If I looked as weird as I felt, everyone in that ice cream shop, giggling over banana boats and strawberry sorbet, would know I was out of my mind and I, frightened now and honest to the bone, said, "Why don't you get the cone, Susan ... I'll wait here ..."

My girlfriend throws me an angelic smile, waltzes away from our lunar module. I am alone, no reference to original me. Panic is sluicing through my body. I'm close to losing it when the car starts to shake. A giant, chrome curtain passes inches from the window and blots out the sun, It's a truck, I know that. A big semi. But in my elevated state I feel the heat of its engine roll over me in sheets. I hear the monster breathing, baboom ... baboom ... baboom ... baboom ... a drumbeat, pumping pillars of smoke out of two chrome stacks, filling my car with its acrid breath. Finally, the engine shuts down with a mind numbing BLAAAAHT, followed by the long hiss of a purging air brake. The cab jerks, then settles in silence. Now I'm seeing every scratch on its steel skin, each speck of dirt, streak of oil, drop of hydraulic fluid. I'm out of control, don't want to be high anymore. I need help.

And I get it; a miracle, a forgotten face, an old friend, someone whose toothy smile, limpid eyes and yellow, daisy chain necklace has never been forgotten. It's Bessie, the face of Borden's Milk, their

Contented Cow, insouciant, full of grace, gazing at me, ten feet high, from the side of this truck.

Bessie was on our dinette table every morning; constant, lovely, in winter and summer, in sickness and in health. Bessie blessed the purity of every glass I ever drank or poured over Mom's sweet morning oatmeal, every cup of hot chocolate before bed. Seeing her again, pillowed by Acid, I go from panic to innocence.

I was rolling down the window, the last barrier to our reunion, when Susan returned, bright eyed and smiling. She slid in, gave me a cone and a cool, wet, strawberry kiss, a kiss so slow and long the ice cream melted. We licked fingers, cooed like nightingales, traded flavors, and kissed again while the cold, buttery liquid slid down my throat spreading its goodness and comfort inside my belly. We were one, we were safe, we could go home.

I almost made it, almost did, but we came to a failed light, a jammed intersection, a traffic cop mastering the mess from the middle. He looks at me, raises a godlike hand, an arrow of energy through my windshield. I make a full stop, we become one, I'm sure of that, his shiny badge, blue uniform, perfect gold braids, center of the universe.

I wait, I am calm. He beckons me forward with a finger. There's a message, it's beautiful, important, hypnotic. I have to touch his graceful, undulating digit. I slip the clutch, hit the gas, stay on mission even as his finger becomes an open hand, an agitated hand, a waving hand whose energy draws me past his fluttering palm to his saucer-wide eyes where there's a new message; *You're going to run over a cop*!

I wrench the wheel, miss him by inches. His terror, my amazement. I look in the rear view, see if he's taking my license number, but he's looking for nothing more than the ground beneath his feet. We are gone. Susan is laughing like a goddess. I join her, wild-eyed, loaded, confident now, taking all challenges. We glide to Dad's backyard, spend hours in drug induced love and honesty. LSD did that. The problem was, when you came down, the world was still the same. As the acid released its grip, my ego returned. I found pride in the accomplishment, tasted the respect I'd soon get. I didn't know LSD had its own pecking order. It wasn't that you took a trip, it was how many trips you took.

# 7
# THE SUMMER OF LOVE

I took a dozen trips over the next few months. Near the end of each one, eternal beauty of the cosmos, I'd call Susan in Montreal and open my heart over the long-distance line. She got fed up, called me out. LSD was the only time I loved her, she said. I drove to Montreal; we'd trip together.

It's winter, I'm at her father's house again, their gray, concrete basement this time, a couple light bulbs and some small rectangular windows, slits really, high up on the wall. We're good, stoned, lots to share. Then I looked at the ceiling and started outlining faces I was seeing in the stucco. Then – and this was fun – I saw them in the door, then the floor, but suddenly, a quick breath, a tremor in my belly. *Maybe I don't want to see any more faces . . .* only I can't unsee them. Even with eyes closed, they're peering back. I'm down the rabbit hole, out of control. *Something's broken, a line's been crossed!*

At any hospital they'd have mainlined a dose of tranquilizers, put me down for twenty-four hours, woke me up on the other side. "Acid was yesterday, Ian." They'd say. "All gone, you can go home now." Only I didn't want to be seen by strangers, exposed, buried under a bad trip. Susan tried to help, but she was high, happy. I thrashed it out in anguish until hours later, the drug released. But Acid's a slow comedown and the whole time, I was relentlessly scanning to see if the faces were gone. Looking for them was the worst thing I could have done. That kept them with me, pulled my hallucinations into the present tense. Now they wouldn't stop.

I knew I couldn't live like this. Within weeks, suicide was on the horizon. I pushed it away, called it, "The last step," kept searching for the next thing to try. I never thought about professional help, which was really dumb. I found if I stayed busy, very busy, I'd get small stretches of peace and that gave me hope so I acted in plays, directed them, worked on cars, helped someone build a greenhouse, took every project I could find because I was beginning to think time might heal this awful state of mind.

One week, I drove to Long Island, fished in the surf for striped bass. That worked too. On the way home, I stopped at Ghost Motorcycles, a big dealer on the East coast. "I'm a mechanic." I said. Anything in the back that's broken?" The guy tells me they have this 650cc, BSA, in boxes.

I see Sal, the owner, offer $200, half of what he wants. Sal puts me on hold, ignores me for hours, but I know he's judging my worth. I go small, eyes down, shopping for pity, just not too much or he'll take me for a loser. I'd have stayed in character a week to get that bike. At the end of our long day, the Pope of Ghost Motorcycles blesses my dream; dispensation to buy those boxes and see what I can do. I scan the parts, but I won't know until I get back to Goddard.

Once there, I lay all the pieces on the floor, lovingly organized. I will build this, set the exquisite timing that sucks measured doses of gas and air into a steel engine block to compress the high-octane mix so a distributor can throw a perfect spark into the sealed space and let the 10.5 to 1 compression ratio turn a thimbleful of gas into a hand grenade with the power to rotate the crankshaft that drives the wheels and spills a pulsing hot exhaust out the chrome tailpipes. I'm gonna build a machine that rockets me over the blacktop and makes those curves feel as smooth as a woman's waist.

A week later I snort speed around 9 PM and get to work. I am meticulous, slow, enjoying every step of the resurrection. At sunrise, I sit astride a white, rolled and pleated seat, cool on my creation. It comes alive, it roars and rumbles and shakes the dorm. I drive my midnight blue baby down the steps, through the front door out to the campus. On Route Four, I hit 75, then 90, then blow through 100 because at 100, the trees on a two-lane blacktop whip by like bullets, the road becomes a point of light, another outlet from crushing loss.

I believe we get maybe ten, true choices in our life. Our other 'decisions' are responses; something goes right or wrong, we don't think, we react. When we're young, some of those big decisions slip by unnoticed, even though they affect us for years to come. Acid and its outcome was one of those. In Montreal, I'd met dance teacher, Elsie Soloman, when Susan took me to a few classes. Elsie, mid-fifties, pushed me hard whenever I showed up. Turned out she was casting for the Montreal Expo; wanted a troupe to do folk dances from around the world at the Canadian pavilion. (Fifty-five million people would eventually visit Montreal, making it the most successful international exposition, ever. "You don't have to audition, Ian," she said. "I'm giving you the job." This was a high profile, straight leap to a creative life, but once again, the only person I was talking to was myself. *Not Montreal. I need a new place, maybe that'll help.* I wish I'd understood the moment, or someone had kicked my butt and said, "Take the job, you idiot!" I walked away. It's something I regret to this day.

Instead, I put the BSA on my Chevy pickup for a drive to San Francisco's, Summer of Love, where the plot to turn America into a giant commune was under way. I leave Goddard a semester short of graduation and take Route 66 through the middle of America. In the 1930s, this two-lane highway brought hundreds of thousands of immigrant families and Dust Bowl refugees, across the country to start their lives over in California.

I made 500 miles a day, drove sunrise to sunset, scared the whole time, frightened enough one afternoon to lay on my truck floor, curled up like a baby, crying, convulsed with fear. One day in Arizona, I had two flat tires within hours. After two flats, there's no spare and I had no help so I started my bike, gunned it off the truck bed to the road, laid the flat across my gas tank and drove to an Esso station where the guys liked my ride and how I brought that tire in so they fixed it on the spot, these strangers, and I remounted it on my bike and remounted it on my truck and fixed the problem and was back on the road, victorious, first time in months. Seems crazy now but somehow, fixing that flat gave me reason to live.

In San Francisco, the sidewalks of Haight Ashbury were full of longhairs in buckskin jackets, girls in flowery dresses. The Grateful Dead had a house there, other bands too, like Quicksilver and Jefferson Airplane. Crowds gathered outside them, hoping to see their idols. I'd go the Fillmore, get high, hear Big Brother and The Holding Company, Country Joe and the Fish, watch people dancing naked in front of our early light shows: oil paints smeared on glass and twirled round on a plate while projecting it onto a screen behind the bands. I moved into a communal house, a rolling group of around twenty people, friends coming and going, sleeping with whoever they wanted. We were thrilled with our revolution.

It all looked good, but San Francisco was already beginning to break its own back, and no one saw it. I watched speed seeping in, parents giving acid to six-year-olds. The streets were littered, ounces of pot became pounds, became kilos, and then someone got killed in a deal gone bad. Nobody outside SF cared about a dead hippy but we did. The first fatality in paradise was a shock, everyone got careful, doors only opened halfway, and what had been given away or traded, now was sold. No one got the real message; long hair and beads don't equal anything except long hair and beads. The retreat had begun. Three months later, I was in Spain.

# 8
# DOWN AND OUT IN MARRAKESH AND TANGIER

The island of Formentera, shaped like a sea horse, was five miles south of Ibiza. A thousand peasants lived there; a spectacularly simple life, fishing and farming without electricity, running water or indoor plumbing. Hippies were right at home. A couple hundred drifted in, rented fincas for a few dollars, got stoned day and night and set up nude beaches and full moon parties. News of the fairy tale spread, tempting stars like James Taylor, Joni Mitchel, and Pink Floyd to drop in, which in turn, brought more weird travelers, finally igniting a stab of resistance.

I was there three weeks when a squad of Guardia Civil came over to sweep the island for longhairs and jail a few for good measure. Formentera's cultural cleansing wouldn't last, not with our impact on the economy. Still, I wasn't going to wait for a knock on the door while the locals were coming to their senses.

A few days later, about to board a freighter in Barcelona bound for the Canary Islands, someone called my name. At the stern were Joe and John, two rock musicians I'd last seen in Cincinnati! We would sail together, graze the Spanish coast, check out the ancient cities of

Valencia and Alicante while our freighter uploaded everything from cork to car parts. It was a lazy week: calm seas, good food, hash sales to the crew. Then we passed the Straights of Gibraltar and plowed into the Atlantic, whose winter swells were huge, I was seasick for three days, only felt better when I stepped off our boat on the island of Gran Canaria: huge, dry, and mountainous, six hundred miles off the coast of Morocco. We found a bus to Arguiniguin, a coastal town we'd heard about on the hippie grapevine. Our ride, top speed of twenty mph, had a floor so rusted we could see the asphalt road, rolling under our feet.

The village's dirt streets were lined with two story buildings of whitewashed stone and concrete, their roofs topped with orange clay, barrel tiles. Blue painted, thick wood shutters on every window, closed during the day, held the heat out and the cool air in. The locals took our money and rented us houses, but their gentle distrust was evident. A young Spanish hippy – Gustavo, gay, when it was still illegal there – told me why. Their civil war had only ended twenty-five years earlier. The winners were still in power, so the surviving peasants – they'd lost their fight for freedom – tilled the soil, ate what they grew and kept their heads down because that's how Spain's tin pot dictator, Generalissimo Francisco Franco wanted it; he had regiments of secret police called, 'The Political Social Brigade.' Step out of line around those folks and jail was the nicest thing that could happen to you.

Franco had been a mid-level officer in the Spanish army when The Popular Front, a coalition of Socialists, was elected to power in 1936. They were idealogues who couldn't make a decision about zoning, let alone national policy and soon, the country was crippled with political paralysis. The rest of Europe, terrified about a "Red" government south of the Pyrenees, didn't say word one when Nazi Germany gave the Generalissimo enough guns and money to start a revolution.

Herr Hitler also delivered planes and pilots and encouraged

Franco – an apt pupil – to try out the idea that terror could go wide. The first control group tested in the science of total war was the civilian population of Guernica, who stepped out of their homes on a sunny, Sunday morning to watch a fleet of planes buzzing overhead, never imagining the bombs inside were for them.

The twentieth century's midwife to mass murder, didn't get his hands dirty on this one; Spain was just cheap real estate to try out strategy and tactics for a world war. By 1939, there had been unspeakable atrocities on both sides, but when it was over, Franco and the Catholic Church had bled the country of students, artists, poets, dreamers, left wing unions, left wing anything.

Hippies like us had a scent of Socialism, but the Spaniards were sure our revolution was harmless. They were wrong. A few years later, their kids would be getting high and when Franco died, it was those children who buried his revolution with him.

We, the rich guys in Arguinuigan, pooled our money, raised $30, and rented a two-bedroom apartment for a month. El Paraiso, the town's only restaurant, served whatever fish the locals netted that morning with a few potatoes and a salad thrown in. What set this village apart was something no other town in the area had; electricity. They'd corralled a World War II generator the size of a tank, proudly put it in the main square. It's dynamo rumbled to life every morning and ran until 10 pm at a speed so languid, every lightbulb in town had a heartbeat. We settled in, abandoned all plans, slept late and slept around. Eventually, I got gonorrhea. The good news about Spain; antibiotics were sold over the counter. At the Pharmacia, a sweet, black haired girl in a white lab coat, quite non-judgmental, sold me penicillin. I asked for a glass of water to take a first pill. She smiled, opened the box, pulled out a glass vial. I needed an injection.

"Donde esta el Medico, por favor?"

"No hay un Medico aqui, Señor." she said, and drew a map to the local health care clinic, which turned out to be a barber shop. In 1150 AD, Pope Benedict banned his clergy from the practice of bloodletting because too many people were dying from the cure. Telling families it was God's will got pretty thin, especially when they'd just watched their priest bungle the job, so the barber's guild—they had experience with sharp objects—took over the trade. That's why their shops still have spiraling red and white posts outside; white for their bandages, red for your blood,

The tin roofed shack I was looking for, stood just a few feet from the ocean. I stepped onto a hard packed, dirt floor in a windowless room, two barber's chairs under sheets. *Just an injection*, I thought. "*What could go wrong?*" At a table near the back, four gents played poker. One of them, early forties, bearded, a wool cap, put his cards down and came over. He read the vial, made a crack to his three amigos. They had a good laugh.

The bearded one walked to a dark corner, returned with what looked like an oversize eyeglass case, a large, steel syringe nestled inside with a needle big enough to drop a horse. He carefully blew the dust off, then punched the three-inch spike into the vial. I turned from my rapt audience, shimmied my jeans to the floor and put both hands on the wall. *This is gonna hurt.* I thought. I wasn't disappointed. He grabbed my ass like a butcher and rammed the needle in. My knees almost buckled with the pain.

When he yanked his drilling rig out of my cheek, I looked over my shoulder. The syringe was in his hand alright, but the needle was still in my flesh. Not missing a beat, he ambled to another corner, returned with a pair of pliers and yanked that spike out like he was pulling a nail. I was speechless, trembling from the hurt. I waved him off, was soon blinded by a white-out which eventually receded when the blood returned to my head. I paid my torturer, limped home and slept that night with an ice bag taped to my ass.

Once a week, Joe, John, and I would grab a rattling bus ride to Las Palmas: a sprawling port city, lively, with coffee bars and cool, shaded patios. We'd hang out there for hours, watch the crowds, or walk the port, looking at ships leaving for other countries while discussing our next move. One day, a tall guy with black hair stepped off a freighter just as we walked by. Holy Shit! It was Mark Pockros, co-captain of the *Kilu*. I hadn't seen him since the day we'd sunk her in Boston harbor. Mark had just been kicked out of Formentera too. He joined us, which was great. I missed his sly sense of humor; he had a joyful grin that let him get away with saying the most outrageous things. One night, he and I, in Las Palmas to hear some live bands, missed the last bus home. It was gonna be a long wait at the station, so we went for a walk. On a residential street, I saw a VW bug, its doors unlocked.

"Hey man," I said. "We're going home!"

"With or without a police escort, Bucko?" Mark replied with a laugh.

I popped the hood, hot-wired the ignition and goosed the gas to drive away. That's when the steering wheel locked with a metallic *thunk*. Whoops, they didn't have that in America! We jumped out to leave the scene of the crime, when I saw an Austin Healey across the street. Those fuckers were even easier to wire, and the Brits didn't have steering locks. All I had to do was reach under the dashboard and bridge two electrical posts with a coin.

"Come on," I said.

"No way," hissed Mark. "Let's get the fuck outta here."

He wasn't laughing now. "Give me one try, man! Hold this," I said, putting a five-peseta coin behind the ignition switch and guiding his hand there to hold it. The dashboard lights went on, the car started alright, but it had a blown muffler and the neighborhood suddenly sounded like race day at Monte Carlo. It was near 11 PM. If the owners were asleep nearby, this night would not end well. A light touch on the gas might have helped, but these cars ran rough when the engine was cold, so you had to keep the revs up. At that point, I didn't care. I hit the gas, pulled away and minutes later we were on the coast road, one eye on the rear view for flashing, red lights. None showed. We laughed like school kids. It was exciting stuff.

We dumped the car outside Arguineguín and walked home. Three days later, the Healey was gone. Mark and I figured if cops came, we'd be on the interview list. Our time there was up. I was broke, but Mark had just got a $50K endowment from his dad for turning twenty-one. He had several thousand wired in. We were good to go. Everything would work out, it always had.

We flew to Agadir. This city, facing the Atlantic on southern edge of Morocco, had been rebuilt after a massive earthquake a decade earlier. Now it had modern apartment buildings, sewers, clean water, electricity. It was the last place we wanted to be. Our goals were about laying back in third world countries, ancient kingdoms, forgotten lands; the few remaining regions on earth with kings, queens, and dictators who wouldn't know a few hundred hippies were living cheap and getting loaded on their turf because almost no one had the nerve to tell them.

Morocco looked right. King, Hassan II held total power, deferred all democracy, kept forty official wives in two dozen palaces. Hassan didn't ride his royal stallion through towns like his father before him, using his sword to behead the occasional subject who got too close. The new King stayed in touch by disguising himself as a working-class Arab, walking the streets, to hear what the nation thought of him. He survived three assassination attempts, one of which ended when Hassan himself, used his shot-up jet's radio, to tell the attacking fighters, "This is the pilot! The King is dead! Let us land the plane!"

Marrakesh was our target, built in the eleventh century on a plain just north of the Atlas mountains and surrounded by sixteen kilometers of stone ramparts. The city had long ago become Morocco's Switzerland; neutral ground where the warring, northern Sahara tribes could meet in peace to sell sheep, leather, silver, gold, and slaves. We heard the old city, the medina, had barely changed since then.

At Agadir's crowded, Centre du Transport, families bunched up on the dirt parking lot, their belongings in boxes and burlap sacks. Men wandered through, selling water and sweets amidst the sulphureous stench of diesel fuel and backed-up toilets. At food stalls, people argued over prices, women led chickens and sheep to the buses and tied them on the roof. Mark got tickets and found our ride. On board, there were no smiles, no welcome, no interest. The men in jellabas stared at us, their women were silent, under full burkas. This was another world.

Eventually, we pulled out to cross the Atlas mountains, the 13,000-foot, fifteen-hundred-mile-long spine that separates North Africa from the Sahara. The narrow, twisting road had no barriers to prevent our bus from tumbling down the cliffs. We threaded between snowy peaks and wild, bouldered rivers, the lifeblood of small farmers and shepherds on both sides of the range. Above the tree line, we swerved from time to time around families of dark-skinned Berbers, herding sheep to market, donkeys too, carrying vegetables and grain. Their women and children wore bright green and orange kaftans. Some carried big clay pots on their heads with large, embroidered leather bags across their shoulders. The men, wrapped in scarves that left only their eyes visible, looked like warriors from another age. At some point, the bus pulled over, we didn't know why until the men stepped off, unrolled prayer rugs, and turned to Mecca.

Around sunset, we landed at a huge square, the Djemaa el-Fna, the traditional entrance to Marrakech's Medina; its endless labyrinth of dark alleys and dead ends. It was like stepping into an ant colony. Thousands of people swilled past, buying, selling and delivering goods and supplies. Women threaded the crowds at a trot, heads covered, elbowing any man who came too close. Haphazard rows of crudely built stalls lit by hissing gas lamps, offered clothes, cheap rugs, and food. Snake charmers, water sellers, madmen, and dancers were there, all drawn to the spectacle and the trade.

The driving beat of drums scudded across the square, the guttural bark of angry commands and arguments over price and possessions, knots of weathered old men, the sharp, unmistakable odor of hash wafting amidst the smell of lamb, couscous, and vegetables cooking on open fires. Children were everywhere. Some of them, selling single cigarettes, would close in on us and yell, "America, America, one dollar!" Others, grotesquely blinded or crippled by poverty or malnutrition, stumbled and crawled, begging for money or food. A man with a tray of hash cookies waved us over. We were soon stoned; Mark found it all funny. For me, getting high only increased the bedlam.

We eventually found the small hotel whose address we'd been given in Las Palmas. A heavyset, olive-skinned woman wearing a yellow blouse and a bright blue head scarf let us in with a warm smile, revealing her gold, front teeth. She locked the big, blue painted door, cutting an avalanche of noise as if a radio had been unplugged. It was wonderful, I felt like I could breathe again in the large, courtyard, centered around a well and surrounded by lemon trees and rose bushes. The second floor was decorated in whorls of orange enamel. Standing on the interior balcony was a brown skinned girl, maybe fifteen, angelic in a soft, white cotton djellaba. She caught my eye for a second, then disappeared.

Mark paid and we went up to our rooms. Mine had a red tile floor, rough, whitewashed walls and hand-hewn rafters. Two bright blue painted windows opened to a landscape of cockeyed roof lines dotted with mosques and spires that seemed, in the fading light, to cascade all the way to the mountains on the horizon. At that moment, loudspeakers erupted across the city, echoing each other's call for evening prayer, one after the other. I closed the shutters, fell asleep under a cheap print of a veiled woman, dancing inside a tent full of men.

In the morning, the square was empty, littered, rank. A few food stalls were opening. I walked deep into the Medina, the only European in its warren of cool, narrow passages. I wandered into sunlit squares whose shops were dedicated to one product; rugs in one, copper cookware in another. I stayed a while in a large plaza ringed by spice merchants; mosaics of brightly colored bins, stacked with fragrant smelling exotics, from cayenne to cinnamon, saffron to sage. A few food carts were there, the women who ran them, haggling over prices with extravagant gestures, in guttural Arabic.

Everywhere I went, merchants called out prices, promises, urging me to come over. Some stopped me in my tracks to pull me in. I was offended, angry. Why did they think I could be hosed over with false smiles and calls to buy? How could they live this way, where life was cheap, poverty a given? I see now that I was passing judgment from a place of privilege. I'd come for this; a powerful energy, unchanged for centuries and the fact was, I couldn't deal with it.

Around midday I found my way back to the Fnah. I ran into Mark, and we went to a café, overlooking the square, filled with druggies, travelers, hippies, gays and lesbians, sharing stories, pairing up, figuring out where to go next and what to see. I ordered mint tea, stuffed with green leaves and sugar, sat on the deck, watching the chaos, the cacophony below.

A week later, Mark left for Beirut. He didn't say anything, but I knew he was fed up paying my way. He gave me some money, but it wasn't long till I began eating at stalls on the Fnah instead of bars and cafes. I got sick, lost weight, began selling drugs, using opium, spinning through the substrates of towns and cities like Safi and Essaouira. Finally, in Casablanca, I traded my fringed, buckskin jacket for three ounces of hash. That was it, there was nothing left.

In January, I took a night train, 250 miles to Tangier, at the northern tip of Africa. For centuries, in peace or war, it had absorbed foreigners and invading civilizations. The Medina, on a hilltop, overlooked the Straights of Gibraltar, a strategic position to see ships long before they landed. Narrow lanes were covered with wood slats, making those passages shady and cool in the summer, but they were cold and wet now, claustrophobic, teeming with people. The smell of burning cedarwood was constant, the rot of sewage too. Arabic music, high pitched, undulating, discordant, blared from radios. Tangier was darker, deeper than any place I'd ever been. I could see how Burroughs wrote, *Naked Lunch* here, and Paul Bowles, *The Sheltering Sky*.

I moved into a cheap hotel for a week, a sleeping bag and the clothes on my back. When the money ran out, I made small scores, slept on hotel floors, sometimes in doorways. I bought a djellaba to cover my western clothes, began wearing cheap, mirrored Ray Bans, staring wordlessly at hustlers, till they gave up and went away. For months, I lived the homeless paradox; this place was hard, things were bad, yet I knew its rhythms, its resources, who to trust, where to get a floor for the night. Europe was only eight miles away, but they had rules, standards, cops, watching out for people like me. I was sure my fall from grace would only get worse over there.

One day, I passed a shop that made wood plates and bowls. Glassy-eyed children, seven or eight years old, were sitting next to lathes whose gears were run by the power of their whirring feet. Deeper in the Medina, my way was blocked by two men, arguing. I'd seen it before, the posturing and preening. But this was Ramadan, the Holy Month, people were fasting during the daylight hours; a soft sacrifice really, but it gave the men permission to lose their minds toward their women, their children and themselves. These two would soon run out of steam, slink off, yelling at each other. I turned down a small alley, passed a shop with used clothing. Hanging from the rafters was a brown, fringed, buckskin jacket, like the one I'd sold in Casablanca.

The shop owner saw me staring, took it down, draped it across my shoulders. He smiled, "Perfect for you, best price, sir, best price." I felt inside the pocket, found the tear I'd made in the seam to hide my drugs. I gave the jacket back, walked away. At a spigot, I bent down for a drink, then thrust my head under instead and turned it full on. The water ran down the stone alley, taking trash with it. *You're gonna die if you don't get out of here.*

I'd been waiting for I'd been in neutral, waiting for the universe to give me an angle, like it always had. Not this time. This time, it was all on me. I took the jellaba off, folded it and left it behind. Outside the British Café, I sold my stash for thirty dirhams, bought a cheap windbreaker and an hour later, my passport stamped, "Sortie du Maroc," boarded a ferry that had seen decades of service between Spain and North Africa. I sat in the airless, overheated cabin. A sudden rain shower sent a family inside, they pulled sandwiches from a basket for their children. The kids, excited about the trip, chased one another, hiding behind benches with shrieks of laughter. One of them left half her sandwich behind. I took it.

The diesel engines revved up; deckhands cast off the ropes. I stepped outside. A mist made for slow going in the crowded harbor, its water, dotted with knots of garbage and seaweed, was impenetrably dark. Broken wharfs and dilapidated buildings appeared through breaks in the fog, small boats rocked at anchor. We motored past the Tangier fortress, centuries old, its huge, black stones, towering overhead. Thick seaweed along the base whipped back and forth as our wake roiled the water, sending a glistening spray over the dry rocks. Minutes later, the boat began to roll. We were passing out of the harbor into the sea. The dirty water and yellow foam was swept away by whitecaps tumbling off transparent, green waves. The air became fresh, sharp with the smell of iodine. There was a burst of sunlight, the heat on my face, it felt like the first time in months. I pulled my collar up, nested and warm. I leaned back against the cabin, closed my eyes. A memory came; a millisecond, the forgotten scent of a spring afternoon, of wood, warmed by the sun, when the universe had saved me as a child. Here it was again. *"You're crossing the Straights of Gibraltar,"* it whispered. *"Centuries of seekers and romantics have been here before you. You will be welcomed."*

Those words were electric, cloaking me in a powerful mythology. Morocco had taken me to the limit. Claimed me for its own but there were gifts here; stories and choices I would understand later. I'd been branded by my journey, and I was proud to have made it. I turned to look back at Tangier. The city, its ancient houses, staggered on the hillside like half opened drawers, was sheathed between a fog above, the Atlantic below, Then the clouds shifted, and just like that, Morocco, all it ever was, disappeared.

Minutes later, a pretty, blue jeaned, black haired, American girl with a knapsack and a sleeping bag, leaned on the rail, next to me.

"That was pretty cool," she said.

"You saw it, those clouds, covering Tangier like that?"

"Yeah, I was on the upper deck. Looking forward to Spain?"

"You have no idea," I said, laughing.

"Where are you going?"

"Might work my way up the coast, back to Ibiza, if things go right."

"You've been there? That's where I'm going! Hear it's great . . . let's get some coffee inside! You can tell me all about it."

"Can't." I said with a smile. "Spent everything I have, getting here."

Jaime was lovely, covered the trip, asked for nothing except our time together. We travelled the Spanish coast, sailed to Ibiza from Valencia. A month later I had the coolest job on the island; sandal maker in the American owned leather shop at the entrance to the old town. Hippies and tourists from all over the world came in, to talk, to get measured up for custom sandals or just listen to our hard-to-find tapes of idols like Dylan, The Stones and Clapton. I was legit, landed, got a regular paycheck. I would score a motorcycle, move to a beautiful house overlooking the sea, meet great women, make friends in Majorca and Barcelona. I got everything I dreamed of when I found the courage to leave Tangier. I didn't know this would be the last year of childhood.

Courtesy of *The Boston Globe*, photo by Bob Dean
Captain Ian Eric Jarvis, run aground at Logan Airport, Boston.

Me, Mom, Mal—six years old, Maine—his pain and mine. We were very different twins who needed each other in very different ways.

Graduation, Junior High, Passaic NJ. Mal, Dad, Mom, Freya, me. Those sharkskin suits, a tribute to Mom's great sense of style.

This pic—unearthing the only insight into my character as a teenager

Georgetown University Sophomore

Two years later, prepping for the draft in Vermont, high on amphetamine

Porsche mechanic, Cincinnati. I only shot heroin on the weekends…

Wheelies in Ibiza—the best, last year of childhood

Old Town, Ibiza, the communal water source in front of the sandal shop

"I'm pregnant," she said. Not the free love I was used to.

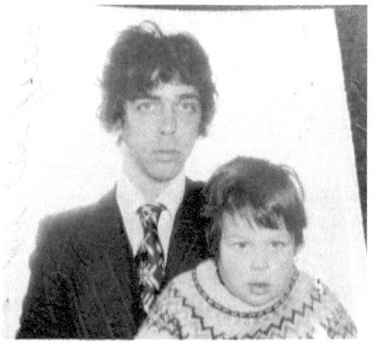

London—Passport pic. Two deer in the headlights.

Our house. First ever. They actually gave me a mortgage

Corsica: temporary cabin I built by hand. No heat, no electricity.

Corsica, Cara in school, all French, all the time

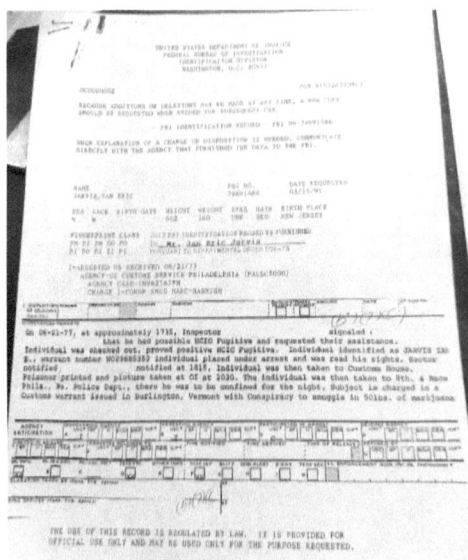

Return to America. FBI charging sheet.

Manhattan.
Making a new life together
Me, starting a career at Saint Gobain.
Cara, after two years without schooling, soon to be accepted at Birch Wathen.

# 9
# RUNNER

Jeff and I were on the I-95, Burlington to Buffalo, the day our lives turned to shit. Three hundred miles into the mission a blizzard rolled up, high wind, black clouds, first flakes sticking to the windshield and the road.

"Looks like the valley of the shadow of death out there," Jeff said, slowing the van down.

"Yeah," I replied, "Long fuckin' way from Ibiza . . ."

We'd been a year on the island, top of the food chain, vanguard of the revolution; a few hundred early longhairs living large on twenty-dollar bills. My job at the sandal shop had given me a great life. After work I'd sit on the deck at my hilltop house, smoke hash under lush, red bougainvilleas, watch small fishing skiffs motor out, their roped lights, swinging over the water like strings of jewels.

There were no fancy hotels yet, no discos, billionaires or cocaine. The peasants lived in small, stone fincas, tended century-old olive trees, and herds of sheep. They sold goat cheese and vegetables in the backyard, cheerfully waving the flies away. Widows, wearing black till they died, came to town in carts, their donkeys high stepping nervously every time a car sped by.

I would've spent a decade on Ibiza's pillow if Bill Frick hadn't shown up. Bill's grandfather, Henry Clay Frick, made millions in the Gilded Age, leveraging larceny, graft, and union busting. In 1919, just before he died, Granddad penanced his crimes by bankrolling museums and charities for the poor. Three generations later, the Frick Foundation, free of all irony, gifted Billy $50,000 just for turning twenty-one.

Moneyed now, he flew in, eager to prove himself at Ibiza's petri dish, every scheme incubated by our community of expats, inebriates and road warriors. Ibiza's Hall of Fame included my neighbor, world class art forger, Elmyr de Hory. His Picasso's and Monet's hung in museums and mansions worldwide. Elmyr, fearless about self-promotion, doubled down on his talents and became an art dealer too; sold his own fakes, which took his duplicity and fortunes, to a new high. He eventually went to jail but only did a few years because most of his victims were too embarrassed to go public about being so badly duped.

Clifford Irving, the journeyman writer who flew in to ghostwrite de Hory's biography, *Fake*, was so inspired by his subject, he stayed on the island to incubate something of his own. After much soul searching, he drew a bead on a monster-sized target; he'd create a fake biography of the reclusive, nutcase billionaire, Howard Hughes.

Cliff bet that once he'd sold his bogus bio to McGraw Hill for a million dollars, once he had best seller status, a *Playboy* interview, face time on talk shows and parties in New York and L.A., that Howard Hughes, living in an oxygenated, glassed off room at Las Vegas' Desert Inn, where he didn't breathe used air or touch anyone, where he was monitored 24/7 by Mormon hustlers waiting for his wasted mind and body to fail and his money to come their way, Cliff's bet was that even after stepping all over Howard Hughes, after forging a made-up life, conjured interviews, faked letters, and publishing those insults for the world to see, that the dying recluse, a stringy wisp of the Hollywood hero he'd been prewar, would not come out of his Vegas cemetery, not step up to a microphone and say with a surprisingly strong voice, that there was no such thing as an authorized, "Damn Lies", biography. When Howard Hughes did just that, he turned Cliff Irving's dream into a criminal landslide, federal jail and a lifelong footnote as the biggest literary scam since the Ten Commandments.

    Billy and I, awed by the hustles, high and high again, decide we're gonna be titans in the drug business. We had plenty of company. A dozen friends, taking R and R on the island, had moved on to Lebanon, Iran, and Nepal and scored enough hash to fund their lifestyle for years. Some got jammed up in third-world jails, but the ones that made it back bought Harleys and houses. They had stories to tell.

    James, who lived in San Carlos, bought a Citroen Deux Chevaux. France's version of a Volkswagen, came with a two-cylinder, air cooled engine so small you could start it with a hand crank. The Deux Chevaux was legendarily dependable; Jim drove his ,4,000 miles to Afghanistan, hired a guy in Kabul to weld a huge metal locker on the roof, filled it with Afghan rugs, clothes, and furniture, then turned around and drove home. At every border, Jim bounced out of his tiny, overloaded car, wild-eyed, laughing, proud to show his inventory. Customs agents in Iran, Syria, Lebanon, and Turkey saw a harmless, slightly crazed, American merchant and cheerfully waved him through. They had no idea, thirty kilos of black Afghani hash were welded inside the roof.

    A woman I regularly got high with in Ibiza called herself Annika. An exotic of unknown origin and indeterminate age, she lavishly decorated her body with jewelry and heavy make-up and prospered by sliding two kilos of hash every few months under a false bottomed bird cage with a deadly, Puff Adder snake, inside. At every airport, the sideways glances went from her teased hair and red, suede pantaloons to her even freakier friend in the cage. That's when lines parted, agents stepped aside, and Annika cruised through customs like a queen.

We wanted our own end run around the system. Bill gave me $5K. I quit my job and took a Land Rover south, across the Straights of Gibraltar to the Rif mountains in northwest Morocco, where they'd been cultivating hash since the sixteenth century. A dealer in Tetuán sells me fifty pounds, invites me home for dinner. Couscous is served. In perfect tradition, his wife shows me how to roll the grains in a ball and eat them off my fingertips, then washes my hands after each course. The dealer, the goodness of his heart, bonuses me a night with their fifteen-year-old daughter. I look her way; she has no idea. I turn him down. In the morning, a risky drive on the mountain road to Fez, where the police sometimes set up roadblocks to nail guys like me. I make it, then take two days in a forest with welding tanks and torches, to build our 'mule'; a dumb piece of 'modern art' on a base filled with drugs.

Next stop is Casablanca, bombed in WWII, then rebuilt; austere, unimaginative, dedicated to commerce with white brick high rises, and concrete office towers. I find a cheap hotel in what's left of the souk; a few ghostly alleys where street vultures sell anything from dope to women. The whores who use my hotel, flirt in Arabic, excited by the tall American on the fourth floor. I pass the time jerking off, morning, noon, and night.

A few days later, the crate's ready. It's time to walk my package through customs. I show up in bell bottom jeans, fringe vest, Nikon camera, cool earring, what could go wrong? Two guys overseeing the sanctity of Morocco's exports stand to attention. They are stunningly unimpressive in their ill-fitting uniforms, but that changes when they mime permission to open the box. I, the shit-scared, picture of confidence, explain my vision, its immutable symbolism. They don't understand a word but eventually, scratching their heads, they put the cover back. I am under no illusions. I should be in jail. This was pure luck.

Our statue is shipping to Canada. Not my plan but in our world, there were no plans, just dreams interrupted by reality, adjust as needed. My idea was to drop a new gas tank in an old VW, stuff it with 20 pounds of hash and weld a two quart can of fuel inside, enough to drive the car off a customs dock in Boston, repeat the routine every four months. Sounded good to me, but our new partner, Pete Weller said, "Fuck that, just send a package to my father's factory in Toronto. Nothing they import gets inspected anymore." We are college graduates, high SATs, all the benefits. Fucking stupid is what we are. A statue from Morocco shows up at the Weatherhead Metal Factory in Toronto. Even if Canadian Customs went blind, was Pete's dad gonna hand it over, no questions asked?

Somehow, the crate had gone through. Buffalo's the last stop in the chain. The snowstorm is gonna make us late, so Jeff hits a pay phone, calls the Customs Office for closing time, comes back shaking his head.

"What?"

"It's a bust."

"What?"

"They said they'd stay open, a fucking blizzard! Guy wanted to know what truck I'm driving, license plate. It stinks."

"Holy Shit!" I said. "We gotta turn around!"

"No way. We came this far. If they follow me, I'll lose them in the back country when I get to Vermont."

I'd known Jeff for years. Great writer, quiet guy, hates risk. Put him in a corner though, he comes out like a rat. "And you're not picking this up," he says, "Your name's on the package."

Jeff drops me off at a hotel in downtown Buffalo. "See you in a while," he promises, but hours later there's no return, no call. Morning television covers a paralyzed city under two feet of snow but nothing about a bust. The streets are feathered, quiet except for the sound of an occasional snow plough grinding by. I'm not waiting for a platoon of cops to blow through that door. I call a cab to the airport even though there are no flights. Two hours later a driver finally shows. I throw my guitar and suitcase in the trunk, slump in the back seat. I'm glazed over, can't get a bead on anything; sure as hell not the cosmic about to embalm the end of my bulletproof life.

That snowstorm, the late taxi, the slow ride, the chunks of time lost to broken lights and blocked streets; a tapestry of seemingly unconnected events that were calibrated in fact, to bring us full stop at a small accident a mile from the airport. The drivers were already walking back to their cars, a minute to wait, sixty seconds to kill, all the time it took to glance out the window at a low roofed motel a block away, a dump no one would notice. Parked in front, its green panel sides resplendent in the snow, was our Econoline van.

I would never have stopped, not *ever* have stopped except for the trail of white smoke pumping out of the van's tailpipe. White smoke meant the engine had just started, it was just warming up. White smoke meant someone's at the wheel.

*That has to be Jeff, he's ready to hit the road. He made it! Fucking unbelievable, he made it!*

I told the cab driver to pull over, watched the scene for a minute. No police cars out there, no people, the place looked empty. Relief swamped my senses, fear disappeared. I told the guy to wait. I stepped out, and took the short walk that changed my life forever.

"Hey, Man!" I said, opening the van door.

Jeff looked at me, stunned. "What, what are you doing?!"

"On my way to the airport, I saw the van. Lets . . ."

"Get the fuck out of here! I'm surrounded by the FBI!"

My mind freezes. I swallow the ridiculous idea I can get out of this if I do what he says. I steady up, close the door, cool walk back to the taxi.

"Wrong van," I tell the driver.

We move on but minutes later, the intercom lights up. He listens, says, "What airline you want at the airport, Sir?" Smart guy. Now they know where I'm going. I gather my hash, pot, and pills, throw them out the window. He drops me at the main entrance, huge building, maybe ten stragglers in the empty hall.

Twenty minutes later, my future shows up; thirtyish, short hair, three-piece suit, small travel bag. The place is empty, but the guy takes a seat near me. Mister personality smiles. He's a teacher, he says, going on vacation.

"Where you headed?" he asks, all innocent.

" . . . Florida."

"That's great!" he replies, with gusto. "Me too. Gotta beat this weather, right?"

FBI boy's having a career moment, but he can't bust me before Vermont tells him Jeff's in custody. Till then, he's a babysitter. I've six, maybe seven hours to break out. Problem is, there's no crowd, no traffic, no streets, nowhere to go. I keep it together, talk weather, Florida, work. I ask about his students. He stumbles over that one, barely a passing grade but we play nice, switch to current events, imaginary families. Eventually I hit the sandwich shop. Five guys sit at a booth in spotless mechanics uniforms. They're all young, white, straight. One of them can't keep his angry eyes off me. *Okay, that's where the reserves are.* I get a coffee which soon sends me to the men's room near the main entrance. Inside, I find that the City of Buffalo, for reasons I will never know, has installed a pay phone next to the urinals. It's a miracle.

I call my brother in Pittsburgh. "Malcolm, I'm in serious shit. I need you to drive to Buffalo airport. When you get here, park in front of the main entrance, come up the steps just enough to show your face. Then get ready to pull out, fast."

"I'm on my way," he says, no questions asked. "I'll be about three hours."

I return to the playhouse, tell story, avoid cynicism, read a paper, hit the bathroom again so my federal fiend gets used to seeing me go. I stay with it till Malcolm appears and we make eye contact. A minute later I smile at my sitter, leave suitcase, guitar and coat, everything I own except my passport and cash, and walk to the bathroom again, only this time, last second, I break right. The 'mechanics' pile out of the café, surround us at the door. They want to throw me up against a wall, turn the day into victory, only they can't. These clowns don't know if I'm CEO of this conspiracy or just the errand boy, but an early arrest would blow everything. They panic, try to goad us into a misdemeanor.

"Hey, you!" one yells. "Stupid Hippies! Longhair assholes!" The others join in. Malcolm, hair trigger temper, raises a fist.

"We gotta leave." I whisper. "Now!"

We make the door, we're out. The wolf pack run for their cars, but they came in under cover.. They parked at the back, they're fucked. Mal and I drive into the night, get a few hours sleep in Pittsburgh. That morning, I call Vermont.

"It's a bust, Ian, everyone's in jail. You shouldn't be on this phone."

"They're not gonna catch me. What happened?"

"They put a tracker on the van, trailed Jeff and arrested everybody. You're the only one left."

I hang up, blown out with worry, but I'm beat. I go back to bed, am half asleep when the mystery voice goes off in my head. "WHAT ARE YOU DOING? THEY'RE AFTER YOU. GET MOVING!"

I wake Malcolm, shower, cut my long hair. I wanted the money, the status, now I'm probably going to prison. I can deal with that, face the madness, find my place. I think there's maybe something noble about being inside. What I can't face is getting busted; a perp walk, cuffs, the humiliation, my name in newspapers, breezy talk about how stupid I've been. What it all comes down to. I'm fighting for pride.

We hit the road like dogs on a fading scent, whipsawing one direction, then another. The bust is on the radio every hour, it's a big deal. "The search for additional suspects continues..."

We don't talk about what's ahead for my brother. He doesn't deserve this. *He's a schoolteacher. I'll tell them he's clean if we're caught but this could still cost him his job, turn his life inside out.* All he did was help when I asked. He put it on the line for me. I'm not sure I deserved it.

That afternoon, we stop at a regional New York airport for a flight to Montreal. I'm almost at the ticket desk when I realize the last thing I want is to turn my passport over for inspection at US and Canadian customs. We go back on the road. I triage every Ford and Chevy that moves in behind us or passes slowly by. *They must have a photo, a plate, a lock on my moves, they're just waiting to see where I lead them ...*

We go south, a PA state highway, two lanes weaving through a string of small towns with neon signs about gas, food, lumber, clothes the beats of a normal life. Around dusk we stop at a restaurant, big place, local winner, red leather banquets, hard-working families, children excited about pie à la mode. Our plump waitress's beehive hairdo twitches like a metronome as she waddles over to brief us on the specials. She asks if we're new to the area... We eat without saying a word.

At the car, I break down, crying like a child, exhausted, bereft, ashamed. I'd been thoughtless and stupid. I'd give to have my life back.

Mal stands by, lets me have this. A siren comes our way. I clock back in. The cop car rushes past.

"Where to, brother? he asks."

I was fed up. "Fuck this" I said. "Let's take our chances at the border."

We hit Canadian customs around midnight, the Buffalo crossing, pretty much where we started two days ago. Mal is at the wheel. I pretend sleep. A uniform on mild alert wakes me up. "Purpose of your visit?" he asks, giving us the old stare down, checking his radar and our nerve. Feels like a long time, but the guy sweeps a hand. "Welcome to Canada," he says. We stay cool, cross the concrete strip. We're out! It's over! I'm elated, I beat the FBI, J. Edgar Hoover, State Police, every one of those assholes! I will have a life, make plans, find good times again!

But soon, the high passes, sadness is more powerful than the gain. All I want is sleep. We find a motel, and next morning, Mal puts his expensive, camel hair overcoat on my shoulders and goes home. It will be a year before the Feds find him and by then, his small part in their debacle would have been more embarrassment than prosecution, they leave him alone.

It's the first day of my new life. I've $100, know two people in Montreal, Susan, my old girlfriend and her cousin, Jason, living together.

"You're not a felon in Canada," they say, when I phone. "Come stay with us."

I train in from Toronto, pivoting between triumph and hurt while the gray sky and flat, snow-covered plains grind by. *This isn't jail, Ian. You're in Canada, not Afghanistan.*

My reprieve lasts four hours. I step off the train, pass a newsstand, see a front page headline; TORONTO HASHISH BUST. $200,000 IN DRUGS SEIZED The Royal Canadian Mounties wanted to bust

Pete in Toronto so the FBI let them keep a few kilos. He's under arrest. I'm next.

I call off my friends, wander for hours through downtown Montreal's huge, underground mall, the world's largest, a city within itself. a brightly lit labyrinth, hundreds of stores, thousands of people. Montreal's French population, the Quebecoise, give the city a second language, another culture, one that bleeds out in signage, food, conversation. It's almost European, especially the French sector of town, a blanket of small homes and narrow streets but it's not much of a distraction when I'm trying to figure out what's next. I find another cheap hotel, have a long walk, wondering if a convoy of police cars will swoop in at any moment and end my run. I take in a rich sunset from Mount Royal, the high park that dominates the city, watch a mother tenderly tuck a scarf around her baby. I see a couple argue, old men talking at a cafe, ordinary moments, but not for me.

A girlfriend in Vermont sends money for a ticket though she knows we'll probably never see each other again. Two days later, at Laval airport, a woman at the Air France desk takes my passport. *This is where she'll ask me to step aside.* She checks the manifest, smiles sweetly, hands the passport and boarding pass back and says, "Sorry Mr. Jarvis, your reservation is confirmed but the flight to Paris has been delayed. It's leaving two hours late."

*That plane's leaving on time*, I think. *She's just calling the troops.* I calm down, walk to the men's room, sit in a stall for ninety minutes. At the departure gate, they take my ticket, just another passenger to get in his seat. I can't fall for it, won't let myself believe I'm out. I board. My heart's racing, throat's dry. I scan the stewardess. Is she looking at me? is there a break in her patter with the others? Are they picking up a phone call from the Captain? Why haven't they closed that door yet? Feels so long, but finally, we pull back and roll to the runway, me, looking out the window for flashing lights, an emergency stop, cops running on board to hustle me off the plane.

The flight goes wheels up. I dissolve in quiet sobs. I've left my life behind. I am a speck of dust, falling on an unknown planet.

## 10
## FUTURE EX-WIFE

At 30,000 feet, the moon's as bright as a flare. I pull the shade, sleep til we land. Lining up for customs at Charles De Gaulle in the morning, a shiver of danger. *Do they know I made that plane?* I pass through, get a taxi to the Champs Elysée. Elegantly dressed people are rushing to work, speaking a language I don't understand. I float with the crowd, pulling in the signals, the vibe, the challenge ahead. I long for a sit down, time alone; I find it at the Café du Trocadero, coffee and croissant while the sun burns off a mist, rising from the Eiffel Tower, glistening across the Seine. I'm empty, crushed, but proud of my escape to this graceful city, hallowed ground that welcomes outcasts and dreamers.

I call Michelle, sweet, shapely, olive skinned. We'd spent a week together in Ibiza, wonder if she remembers. She invites me to her place in Neuilly, paid for by a Swiss industrialist who visits a few times a year. Michelle's lovely; her embrace is true. In the morning, she makes it clear she's happy to have me there, no matter what. I'm cocooned, I sleep late, walk for hours, from the Louvre to Bastille, from Sacre Coeur to Montparnasse. I stop at tiny, artisanal, shops, generations of ownership; a violin maker, custom framers, a courtyard where they sell old fashioned brooms and brushes. Every morning, outside our local boulangerie, a line of people wait to pick up freshly baked baguettes while a warm, buttery smell wafts down the street. Paris feels soft, confident, licking its own popsicle. Food and drink are cheap, making love is a nightcap, they don't look under rocks here.

But it's winter, so many days are cold, gray. Worse, I feel the spine of every great city; an unyielding demand to be relevant. I don't speak French, don't have a work permit and anyway, who has skills, a degree, a trade, a vision. At this very moment, my friends in Vermont are surely out on bail. They have goals, they're muscling up the resources for a fight in court. (A battle they will lose. They are eventually sentenced to seven years in federal prison.) I keep reliving the bust. Would I have been better off to take that ride with Jeff? Could I have changed the outcome? Maybe I'd have opened the package in the truck, seen the tracking device, walked off with it through the woods or tossed the hash to pick it up later. I can't let go of the idea I might have saved it I'd stayed.

Michelle's face floods with disappointment when I tell her I can't stay, but she stands down with grace, buys me a first-class ticket on the night train to Barcelona, where the ferry to Ibiza, crosses a calm sea, under billowing white clouds. In port, I pass fishermen and their crews, repairing nets on the quay. From the heights of the old town, red roofed fincas, surrounded by palm trees and terraced farms, radiate across the plain. Low, forested hills stand in the distance. A mailman bicycle's past. Women sprinkle water in front of their doorways to keep the dust down. I feel good, think the worst is over.

I'm wrong. My paydown is just beginning. To guide me to the catacombs of my life, the universe sends a shepherd: Sophie Rendell, a tall, lanky, British subject, a decade older with two, beautiful, blond-haired children, Steven 7, and Joanne 12. Sophie's had a chaotic life and in our world, that's a turn-on. She brought her kids up in Italy,

Germany, and the US, left them in one of those places for months, to walk to the base camp of Mount Everest. She took them to Greece and hung out with mercenaries, hippies, and artists like Leonard Cohen. Now she was here, her life as fluid as mercury.

I'm the perfect age to imagine buffing up my self-esteem with an older woman whose children somehow seem to be a bonus. I thought Sophie's survival rested on her wits and courage, and it had, but there was a side I didn't see; she was a world class manipulatrice. Two days after we had sex, she moved in. The quarantine began immediately. Why was I spending time with friends? Who were these other women, had I slept with them too? I was on the wrong side of her temper as well, and by the end of our first week, I was wondering what I'd gotten into. That's when she hit me with a paralyzing takedown.

"I'm pregnant," she says.

I stare at the whitewashed walls of my finca.

"Isn't it wonderful?" she adds, her face glowing.

I manage a thin smile, hope she's full of shit but Sophie, a three-baby veteran, not only knew her cycle, she knew the flutter of adjustments her body made the moment my sperm began busting her chromosomes. I was stunned. Free Love was a pillar of our revolution, but it was backed up by birth control pills. Everyone knew that, everyone used them. My new girlfriend changed the rules and didn't tell me. I had no say in her decision. To this day, I find that incredible.

I think we try to fix as adults, what we couldn't fix as children. When we marry one of our parents, we're trying to re-invent the world we painfully failed, hoping we'll get it right this time. I know it's what I did. On top of that, I'd been annihilated by the bust, was weak in all ways. I didn't say a word when the spring-loaded narrative went off; I was going to be a father.

We were so new together I wasn't even sure this child was mine.

Sophie told me she had to fly to London to have the baby. I would follow in my 1958 Citroen, with her two surviving children and everything else we suddenly shared. She took the plane and three weeks later, we took the ferry to Barcelona. The car, in synchronicity with my life, blew up outside Paris so we wound up at Dover customs with three duffle bags and $35. It's not like our passports matched, but the guy believed me when I said their mother was waiting in London. He reluctantly let us in with one-month visas and we took a train to Charing Cross and a cab to Hornsey Lane, in Highgate; a quiet, treelined area next to Hampstead Heath where Sophie was sitting a friend's apartment. My tip to the cabby was so small, he gave it back.

*I can't do this*, I thought, watching Joanne and Steven walk to the building. *This can't be my life*. I'd already said those words a hundred times in my head, but telling Sophie meant being truly, deeply, magnificently selfish. I didn't have that kind of loyalty to myself. I followed her children inside. A few days later I began trolling for work, but without a labor permit the wages of my sins were low paying jobs in construction and restaurants. I was soon making just enough money to keep us in food, though I remember one afternoon, the fridge was empty. Sophie phoned some old friends, gave it a high energy, "Can't wait to see you" conversation, until they invited us to dinner. The smell of chicken and brussel sprouts wafted through their apartment for what felt like hours of happy talk. I was hungry. All I wanted to do was eat!

At the end of the month we'd be homeless. Sophie was pressuring me to marry. Then I could apply for residence, she said, end my illegal status, have a legit job, a way to stay in England. *Stay in England? Stay in fucking England?* I wanted sunshine and sea. I wanted drugs and girls. I wanted to rebuild *my* life, not hers. She didn't stop coming after me though, and one morning, we took a bus to Haringey, Town Hall, where my sad-eyed stepchildren watched a civil servant read the rules and regulations of a lifetime relationship. I slipped a borrowed wedding ring on Sophie's finger and said, "I do."

My internment in the British Isles had officially begun. The next day I ran an ad in a dippy, alternative newspaper, *The International Times*:

HIPPIE MECHANIC LOOKING FOR FREE,
DEAD CARS TO RESSURECT.
*Abandoning your car? Call me. I'll take it away.*

I heard from people whose automobiles were broken or stuck on the street, or rusting in the backyard; relics nobody wanted but me. I'd worked a deal with a London junkyard. If I delivered registration papers and the address; he'd give me £10 for each one. Soon, among the rejects, I found a Volkswagen bus that needed a new cylinder head. That one was a keeper. I pulled the engine and rebuilt it on the street. Now we had wheels, maybe I could get something going. First, however, I had to learn how to drive on the wrong side of the road. My second day at the wheel, I was flowing with traffic, I was fine. Then I took a left turn to a new street and was stunned to see another car coming right at us, seconds from a head-on collision. *What the fuck? Doesn't he see I'm here?* Then I realized it was me in the wrong lane! I swerved of course, his horn blasting as he went by, but that image, the car bearing down, its driver I imagine, praying the asshole in front of him would wake up, I never made that mistake again.

I still had to learn how to cross a busy street though. One day, I stepped off the curb on Edgewater Road, looked to my right, and saw the back end of cars, moving away. My brain converted that image to, *No cars coming*, and I stepped right into oncoming traffic. A lively conversation went down between myself and the guy who locked his brakes to avoid running me over. (I found out later, looking the wrong way is how a lot of Americans go home in a box,)

There was a fashion blitz going on in London; belts worn outside sweaters and coats. I was sure, with my sandal making experience, I could turn those belts out, maybe have a business. Sophie scoffed at the idea, told me I should get a regular job, but we were a couple who'd already stopped listening to each other.

In London's East End, I found a company that sold leather tools. The owner there suggested a small family-owned, tannery on Ratcliff Cross Street, Wiggins Thomas and Rudd. Mr. Thomas III, sold me—one time only, he said—a quarter skin. I'm sure they thought I'd never be back. I had tools, I had leather. Now it was time to scour antique shops for old buckles. A week later I'd produced a dozen belts, each one with a unique buckle. I'd charge high prices, make high profits.

The family piled into our unlicensed VW for a drive to London's version of NYC's, Fifth Avenue; King's Road. That street, a good mile long, was the center of the city's avant garde, clothing scene. Mary Quant started there, taking advantage of a UK law that didn't tax children's clothes. She designed women's skirts that were short enough to meet 'child size' dimensions. That 'look', both shocking and untaxable, launched the Mini Skirt revolution. In no time, small, independently owned shops occupied every available space on Kings Road. The Beatles bought clothes there, The Stones too. The sidewalks were crowded with people my age in bell bottoms, Edwardian shirts and blouses with high collars and puffed sleeves. It was my crowd, my time. I was sure these belts would sell.

I parked at the south end, near a traffic circle. Sophie and the kids waited while I began the first business of my life. I was all hippie: shoulder length, curly hair, sandals, blue jeans, and a blue work shirt. I even carried my belts in a straw shoulder bag from Ibiza! Walking into stores, I was met with quizzical looks, daunting looks, friendly looks, but one way or another, got turned down at every shop. The bottom line; if stores bought a design, it would be in six sizes across two colors. I wasn't selling anything at retail with one-off buckles, no matter how interesting they were. As bad as that turned out to be, the day wasn't a complete bust; a store clerk bought a belt for five quid. With that money, I put gas in the car and bought an order of fish for my pregnant wife. The kids got the chips.

There isn't a business venture I haven't started in which I wasn't certain of success. That innocence has worked throughout my life because on the many occasions I've been knocked on my butt, I get up again and do exactly what I was always going to have to do to make my dream come true; don't worry, put one foot in front of the other.

I borrowed £50 from Sophie's parents and a week later, disguised as a regular guy in short hair, slacks, cheap shoes, and a clean shirt, I again went to King's Road, this time carrying a fake leather, black case with twelve new belts inside. The saddlery buckles I showed were available in the hundreds from a supplier in Goldens Green. *Yessir, you want forty-eight belts across these two designs, no problem!*

That day, I made my first sale; three dozen belts at £2 each. The average weekly wage in the UK was £20, a nice apartment rented for £30. I'd just earned £72. I didn't know I was one of the first people in London to convert solid brass horse buckles into a fashion statement. I just knew I was on to something. A week later, I delivered the order; beautiful, top grain leather, hand finished, lovingly assembled. The customer was impressed, my invoice was cheerfully signed.

"We'll get a check to you in thirty days." The manager said.

"Pardon?"

"Sorry, that's how it's done. You didn't know?"

I'd just taken a big order, sixty belts from Take Six, a London chain on Oxford Road. I needed to get paid now, to buy more raw materials for my new client. It didn't feel right to go back to Sophie's parents even though I'm sure they would have helped. Instead, that Sunday, at 4:00 AM, I drove to Bayswater Road, a wide, leafy street on the north side of Hyde Park that's bordered by high, wrought iron fencing. Behind those railings are 150 acres of open, tree lined space, where Londoner's could walk, picnic, exercise free speech, and ride their horses too. It's a lovely escape in the middle of the city, and on weekends, that Bayswater sidewalk became a mile long market. Crafties, dreamers, the underemployed, hung anything they had on the wrought iron fencing; found objects, antiques, clothes, Elvis posters, used books, velvet paintings of dewy-eyed children. I was going to be part of it.

It was pitch black when I got there but people were already roping off their sectors, greeting friends, sharing coffee. Energy and excitement were in the air. I walked the street till five feet of unused railing turned up and just like that, on a Hyde Park sidewalk, I had a store. The day turned out well, I sold eight belts for 48 quid! Take Six would get their order, the company would survive. I returned to Bayswater every Sunday for three months, until cash flow caught up to sales. I was building a business.

The city, so dense, so full of architecture, monuments and history, was a fascinating place. At first, I was awed by Big Ben, Parliament, Trafalgar Square, Soho, and Carnaby Street. One afternoon I even stopped at Buckingham Palace to see the changing of the guards in their red tunics and busbys. Now, as I worked like crazy to make sales, those places just became markers, passages, or detours in my growing knowledge of the city's streets and how to get from A to B in record time.

I was to find, when I lived in Paris, that the fastest way anywhere in that complex city, was to drive the big avenues, because the small ones were blocked with trucks making languorous deliveries to the ateliers, bars and tabacs on every block. The opposite was true in London. Speed to my targets relied on an intimate knowledge of small, side streets. Avoiding the big ones was important because they were forever backed up with excessive traffic. A tight schedule and spirited approach were a proving ground for my driving skills. I was pretty good, but eventually I had an accident, one that illuminated England's age old, class struggle. I was at the wheel of my rocket ship, just behind Harrod's back door, sometimes used as an exit for the rich and famous. A chauffer driven Mercedes swerved at high speed around a double-parked Bentley and crashed into me. Half a dozen of the well-heeled stepped out to hand the driver their card. I was in a VW, no one came to my window.

 A growing business made me a good client at Wiggins Thomas and Rudd. They were great. The head tanner, Steve, went the extra mile for my growing orders which invariably, were far more diverse than the standard black, wine, or brown. Wiggins gave me greens, reds, blues, every color I could offer clients to keep trendy boutiques excited about my designs. People liked me, were attracted to the big buckles I used, and in some cases, designed. I delivered quality products, created strategies to brand my company. I built good relationships, made mistakes but took responsibility, and fixed them. I was creating a real company, a new life, something to feel good about. (That guy who interviewed me at Georgetown had been right!)

 What I couldn't fix, was my marriage. True or not, everything Sophie did and said began to feel like manipulation. I didn't know how to control her temper either. I'd wake every day hoping we'd have our argument in the morning. I learned to apologize early and often, anything to keep the peace. Years later, I would understand how her childhood victimized her, imprinted the constant feeling, she was on thin ice.

Growing up in London during the war and the Nazi blitz, her generation ditched school, ignored adults, laughed at the rules because they saw no order to things. A fresh orange was a lottery prize, death came the same way. Forty thousand Londoners died from bombing raids, unexploded ordinance and Nazi missiles. A thousand families a day got telegrams saying their husbands and sons were missing or killed. No one knew how, or when this would end.

The war made madness ordinary, and it didn't end with peace. There were years ahead before the rubble cleared and buildings were rebuilt and broken hearts began to mend. Sophie's parents ran a pub; she helped at the bar but with puberty, she turned to sex. Sophie was eager, multi-orgasmic, men paid attention. Fucking became an escape, then a currency. Now, after two decades hopscotching from one country to the next, a divorce, the death of her third child, a life rattled by insecurity about money, people and love, I think it left her deeply conflicted; she wanted freedom, but she craved stability.

I see now that controlling me wasn't really the goal, controlling her life was. She protected herself and our unborn child the only way she knew; by keeping me small and sequestered. Jarvis Belts made money. We rented a two-bedroom flat in our Hornsey Lane building. Down the hall was Steve Broughton, who would, a few years later be known in music history as the drummer on a seminal album titled "Tubular Bells." At the time though, he was playing with his brother in a very popular UK group called the Edgar Broughton Band. I'd learned a little guitar in Ibiza, had written a song, and one day I played it for them. The next week they took me along to hang out at Abbey Road Studios, heard me improvising harmonies while they were editing tracks. Steve asked if I wanted to go with them to a performance in Manchester.

There were no promises, no stated interest, but when I put it to my wife, rather than support the man she married, I was shamed instead. "Why would you do that?" she said. "You don't want to hang out with those people . . ." I didn't have the spine to stand up for myself, turned the Broughtons down. They didn't ask again. Throughout my marriage, I never had a friend, someone to hang out with, share a beer, tell a story, have a laugh.

Cara was born in January, a day before my own birthday. I took Sophie to Charing Cross hospital the night before. She was admitted to a ward with other women waiting to give birth. Her doctor kept stopping by to check but she didn't dilate, and the baby just didn't drop down. Sophie was there about fifteen hours, me, sitting by the bed. Suddenly, she said, "It's happening, now!". It was so fast, they didn't have time to transfer her. A passing doctor was pulled off the hall, he made the delivery standing next to Sophie. No one even thought to get me out of there, so I watched the entire birth from the foot of the bed – this was a time when men weren't even allowed to be present, much less get the best view in the house. I saw Cara's head appear, her shoulders, saw her gasp for air and cry. One look, you knew who the father was.

We left Charing Cross the next day, had an argument before we got in the car. Cara didn't ask to be part of a ghostly marriage any more than I had. I would take care of my daughter; I took care of everyone, but I was buried emotionally, running it by the numbers, not the love she deserved. All I could do, was default deeper into work.

I soon drove a new Land Rover and Steven was in private school. Two years after stepping off the ferry at Dover, I walked into a Westminster Bank branch in Hastings-on-Sea; we'd found a wonderful, house there to buy. The branch manager, who had the power to grant that loan, asked a lot of questions. I did my best but walked away knowing he'd never say yes. I didn't even have tax filings. A week later I came back for the answer, ready to tell him what an A-hole he was but when we sat down, he smiled, slid a document across the table and said, "Sign here, Mr. Jarvis." I had just bought a house, two years after landing in England with $35 to my name. Months later, over a drink, Norman told me why he approved the mortgage.

"You had nothing. On paper, your loan was the biggest risk I ever took. I did it for two reasons. First, there was something about you. I felt you wouldn't let me down." He chuckled.

"What?"

"The second reason?" he replied, laughing again. "I was retiring. If I fucked this up, it wasn't going to be my problem!"

Norman, by way of the only mutiny in his entire career, had green lit us a lovely, four-story Regency home in Hastings' charming, old town. 21 Croft Road looked over a tree filled, church yard. From the top floor, you could see the English Channel. Most mornings, I would take Cara to the beach, only a few hundred yards away. I'd tie a rope round her waist and secure it to my wrist. Then, exhausted by the responsibilities and work, I'd fall asleep, awakened repeatedly by a tug on the line as she gamely tried to walk into the sea!

I turned the large, windowed, concrete shed in our backyard into our production studio, bought machines and set up the tables and racks to hand produce hundreds of belts a week. I would be at it twelve hours, then cut more blank belts on the dining room floor for the next day's work. I drove to London weekly, to buy raw materials and make sales. The business was growing, we were even exporting to Europe. I'd built a life for five, yet I couldn't escape the frustration of a failed marriage. I was a decade younger than my wife, as close to her daughter's age as I was to hers. I had no experience as an adult and was surely an uninspiring partner for Sophie's escalated sexuality. She wanted me to do things to her that didn't turn me on, not at an age when my horizon began and ended pretty much at the first point of entry.

In the fourth year, wiped out by isolation, I booked an overnight trip to London, took a tall, sweet salesgirl to dinner, was invited to her apartment. I would sleep with this woman, know her smell, feel her breasts against my chest, her perfect, white skin. It was beautiful, tender, I closed my eyes in anticipation; I could hardly wait to be inside her, but the moment our lips touched, I spun instead, into a long forgotten, child's memory.

*I was eight years old when I first saw The New York Times headquarters on Broadway; awestruck by a giant electric sign that encircled the building. On it, what looked like a million lightbulbs, were flashing in controlled patterns to create world headlines in letters fifteen feet tall. It was mesmerizing, but what made that sight indelible was the fact that somehow, somewhere, someone was magically making those bulbs light up in sequence so that each announcement, slithered around the building like a snake.*

JAPS SURRENDER<br>
TRUMAN WINS PRESIDENCY<br>
CHINA INVADES SOUTH KOREA

And on this night in London, about to cheat on my wife after four years, I see that New York Times board again. There's a message. It's for me.

THERE GOES YOUR MARRIAGE.

My eyes snap open, I'm shocked, not sure what to do. Thankfully, the young woman in my arms has no idea what just happened. In the morning, I drive home, certain I have a different vibe, a look, something Sophie will see or feel. I walk in the door. Lunch is ready. There's no price to pay. Not yet.

# 11
# LIVING DANGEROUSLY IN CORSICA

I cashed out of England a year later, fed up with my life. We sold the business, the house, packed everything, moved to Corsica; a verdant, French island in the Med, a hundred miles south of Nice. You could look up from the beaches there and in the distance, see the snow covered, craggy peaks of the island's mountainous interior. Corsica's west coast was magnificent. (The French call it the savage coast.) It was sparsely settled, but wherever the miles of rocky cliffs gave way to a protected harbor, there was a charming village with fishing boats on the beach, and houses stacked up on the hills. We'd bought an acre of land on the other side of the island, where the terrain was gentle, sloping. Most of Corsica's population lived there, amidst farms, vineyards and two of the islands three cities, Bastia and Porto Vecchio.

We were excited. After four intense years, we'd returned to the island life; laid back locals, slow days, no hassles. It looked perfect. Maybe changing zip codes *could* do some good. Our property, five miles south of Porto Vecchio, was in Palombaggia; a spectacular beach, whose open, blue waters were only a few hundred meters from a line of low hills laced with pine, olive and chestnut trees. We would build a dream house on those hills, an open view across the Mediterranean to Sardinia.

Almost every other island in the Med is arid and barren. Corsica is still green and lush because the Phoenicians, Greeks and Romans couldn't plunder it for the endless supplies of wood they needed to build ships. The Corsicans never surrendered, they had their glorious mountains to retreat into and continue the fight. The highlands were called 'Le Maquis', and during those centuries, Corsican men also escaped there after they'd killed someone in the local blood feuds that could last for decades. I didn't speak French, didn't know any of this, didn't know Napolean was born on the island, that the Corsican mafia was a criminal power all over Europe. I didn't know Corsica's brutal legacy of violence and tribalism had become a tradition so enduring that France had long ago, refused to let the locals be cops on their own island. It didn't take long to find out. I sell my car to a guy in Solenzara, says he'll pay the remaining $400 in two weeks. I show up on the promised day, the asshole pulls out a pistol.

"How much do I owe?" He says, glassy eyed, stinking of liquor.

"Not a penny." I reply, and walk away, the muscles in my back, tight as a drum.

A month later, building a small, temporary house on my property, I rent a cabin from Jean Luc, nice man, doesn't mention that two families from different villages are fighting over what he calls, *his* property; a small house in a very expensive area called Calla Rosa. It's winter, so the big homes are largely unoccupied and my rental there is as good for him as it is for me. I return from dinner one night, light up half a dozen guys in my brights. It feels edgy but I park, walk the gauntlet. One of them, short, a round face, high forehead, Napoleon's DNA, asks,

"Who are you?"

"I'm staying at Jean Luc's cabin," I reply, helpfully pointing it out.

"*Jean Luc's* cabin?" Napoleon screams. "*Jean Luc's* cabin!!"

And just like that, everyone pulls a shotgun from behind their backs. Shorty slams his in my chest, yelling in the Corsican dialect. I don't need a translator, I know by now, he can pull the trigger, make his name and I disappear, no trace.

"Calm down, Sir." I say in my meager French. "I have nothing against you."

My uber sincerity only makes it worse. He's furious, shoves me to a wall, waving the shotgun in my face. The guy is losing his mind and I'm not the only one who knows it. Two other bandits step in and walk me away. Napo gets a last word in though, in French, so I understand him. "Monte dans ta bagnole!" He yells. "Si tu bouges tu es mort!". (Get in your car. If you move, you're dead!). I'm marched to the VW, guards with guns on either side. I sit between them in silence, trying to take their temperature. "Have to pee," I say. I'm not lying. They give me the old gallic shrug, walk me to the bushes, shotguns casually draped in my direction. I'd like to say I had a long, loud, prideful piss. I didn't. I was mind fucked, my full bladder wouldn't give me relief, not now, not in front of these guys. I scavenge a scrap of pride; don't wait for them to make the call. With a sigh, I put my dick away and zip up. Tweedle Dee and Tweedle Dum have a laugh. *Maybe that's a good sign. They wouldn't think it was funny otherwise, right?*

I'm back in the van when suddenly, everyone throws their guns in the bushes. A minute later, two gendarmes on patrol drive up. I have options here. I take none of them. I drop below the dashboard while the boys explain what they're doing late at night around so many closed houses. They must've said something right because the cops motor on. Keeping my mouth shut gets me props. A guard leans in, says, "This isn't about you, just sit still." *That is definitely a good sign . . .*

Then, no warning, an ear-splitting explosion. Pieces of Jean Luc's cabin land on the VW's roof. That's when cars, unseen until now, roar into the parking lot, doors open. The wrecking crew jumps in, cars squeal away.

I'm alone. At least I hope so. Has someone been left behind to deal with the witness? I slowly move a hand to the ignition, start the car, look around. It's still quiet out there, so I put the VW in gear, leave without haste - wouldn't want anyone to think I had something to fear. I make it to the main road and sleep that night, a free man.

In Porto Vecchio the next afternoon, people say, with shit eating grins. "Hey Ian, the cops are looking for you." I'm the only American living on this half of the island. *Damn, the gendarmes must've recognized my car*. I turn myself in. They take me to a small room, talk this crime, that crime and finally, my crime. These assholes tell me I'll be okay if I identify the men. I go for humor.

"They all looked like Napoleon . . ." I say.

That one lands like a brick, but we both know I'll wind up buried in some valley if I expose even one of those guys to prosecution.

"Way too dark, didn't see their faces."

It's a standoff. They put me in a room, make me wait, came round again, same questions, same answers. Finally, fed up, "Fout le con!" they say. "Get the hell out of here." A week passes. I don't hear from the demolition team. There's no retribution, no warnings, everyone knows the score.

These are cool stories now, about luck, maybe courage, but they are really metaphors. I wasn't on this time warped island to save my marriage. I was there to kill it, the way men and women have since the first fire turned caves into homes; by fucking the next-door neighbor.

My exit strategy, my cure, twenty-three-year-old, Marie Paoli, walks over one day with her boyfriend to say hello. Marie is a wildflower, half-Corsican, half-Italian, long blond ringlets, a perfect, hourglass body and bright, blue eyes with one message: "No rules." I'd find out later she'd been a heroin addict at sixteen, did time in jail, had a daughter she left with her grandparents. I only knew she was stunning and open, and our energy was unmistakable. Flirtations begin, sideways looks, a word, a touch, a dance around my wife's suspicion that goes on for months. Yet with all of it, so awkward and transparent, I'll always believe Sophie was the first to know and chose to be the last to find out.

Marie and I eventually engineer a weekend behind all backs, an escape to the mainland on separate flights. That afternoon we screwed in the back seat of a Renault, north of Cannes. We were a hundred miles from her man and my woman but there was nothing sensual about it. I was petrified, fucked her like a rabbit, don't know why she let me near her again, but back in Corsica, our sex became a marathon. I'd make love with my wife at night, leave in the AM, screw Marie in her room, in the woods, the ocean, the beach, on shop floors, up against doors. Our affair was as discreet as an air raid, but I couldn't stop. I was alive.

And terrified. For Marie, my song was simple; our life would begin when I told Sophie at summer's end. That worked in March, but now it was August. I'd become a Wikipedia of double talk. Marie was exasperated with all the reasons why I couldn't yet tell my wife. Sophie was pushing back hard on my endless excuses to go to town, stay in town, get home late. My strategy came down to praying something would happen to my wife before it happened to me.

I was fighting for time but the universe eventually takes care of scheming bastards. Marie and I are in Porto Vecchio one night, walking the harbor, eyeing the rows of gleaming yachts riding lightly at their berths. We envied the bright eyed, tanned crews. We would join them soon, have no fixed address, no boundaries. We were inside our dream, arm in arm, when I heard an angry voice echo down the high road leading to the harbor. "You piece of shit! You son of a bitch! I'm going to kill you!!"

Sophie was driving our car headlong through the crowd, surely high with relief that she could finally give her suspicions the workout they deserved. I had it coming, but I would not be punished in front of strangers. I jumped on my motorcycle to lead my wife out of town, leaving Marie behind because of course, Sophie would follow. It was me after all, who committed the crime, orchestrated every moment, manipulated and fucked her while still wet with Marie's juices. Who would let a man escape that?

A woman would, especially if she blamed his mistress, because women know that men are stupid and only a piece of garbage would steal a man since stealing a man is like taking candy from a baby. Sophie's dream was to kill Marie, not me. In the end, it was only the crowds, gawking at the spectacle, that kept my wife from strangling my girlfriend and crushing her beautiful breasts under our car. I saw none of this. I was alone on a hillside, tuning up a list of excuses. Eventually, an emissary arranged a meeting. I made it to the rally point that morning, a coffee shop on the edge of town. I was exhausted, ashamed. If Sophie had just taken me home that day, I might have slipped back into our misery.

We started okay, talking quietly, just between us. But her voice rose, it began drawing people's attention.

"Not here," I whispered, looking at the crowd. "Please, not here..."

"Not here, you asshole?" She yelled. "Not here? You weren't too worried about dragging your mistress around in public, were you?"

And she punched me in the face with all the might and frustration any woman would. The worst had happened; a public hanging, exposed as a fraud. That terror had driven emotional cowardice since childhood, yet in this extraordinary moment, the trap door under my feet didn't open, it disappeared in rage, a landslide, cut loose by years of pressure and confusion, duty and submission. The whole edifice gave way, and for the first time in my life, I didn't care what anyone thought.

"Don't you get it, you piece of shit! I screamed, "We're finished! Do you hear me? "

I stormed off to the car. Sophie followed, I let her in, no idea why and drove away, not a word between us. Time to cool off maybe? But a mile down the road, she slugged me again. I pulled over, reached across to her door, put my feet on her hips and kicked her out.

"You! Will! Never! Screw! With! Me! Again! not another fucking minute!" I yelled, and drove away. An hour later, I had escaped to Le Maquis too, near Corte. I took a room in a village hotel, bought a couple of baguettes and cheese and dropped into a two day coma. When I came up for air, I saw the razed ground, the wreckage, my daughter, left behind in that mess. But the words had come. Nothing would get me back. I drove north to Bastia, boarded a night ferry to the mainland. The boat pulled away and motored into the Med, its white wake undulating across the swells like a dog's tail. I wasn't scared anymore. Anger was my fuel, thickening my armor, concealing all guilt. As Corsica's craggy, mountainous profile disappeared in the darkening sky, I slipped my wedding ring off and threw it in the sea.

## 12
## LET LOUCHE IN PARIS

Marie met me a few days later in Nice, a lovely city. Small, brightly colored homes and buildings line its quiet streets, narrow lanes and open-air markets. The beachfront esplanade, lined with palm trees, stands in front of fine, historic hotels; stories to tell about famous people, great events. A broker showed us a studio during France's two-hour lunch break, which covered the fact that the street in front, Avenue Gambetta, was a major trucking artery out of Nice. The noise, day and night was bad, but the smell of diesel fumes was worse. A week later, we gave notice, we'd leave at the end of the month.

I got a job at a Volkswagen dealership behind the Hotel Negresco. Each day after work, I parked my VW on the avenue, didn't realize every cop in Europe believed those vans, especially those with Dutch plates like mine, were mules for the drug trade from Lebanon to Morocco. I got the news early one morning on my way to work; six men in suits coming up the wide staircase.

*Who are these guys? This place, this hour?* Following local custom though, I drop a warm, "Bonjour Messieurs."

The leader, a gaunt man with eyes as cold as an owl, hears my US accent, barks, "Arret Monsieur!"

"Is that your blue Volkswagen van, parked outside?"

I nod.

"Come with us." says his lieutenant, clamping a hand on my arm to steer me upstairs.

This is not good news. I'd just bought – first time in five years – half an ounce of hash. *How does that rate an undercover squad? Doesn't matter, these cops find my fifteen grams, I get processed in, a routine wire is sent to Interpol, I go on a free flight to NY and into the arms of the FBI.*

"My girlfriend's inside." I say. "She has the keys."

I'm lying, but they don't check my pockets. I knock on the door, yell in alarmingly weird English, "Hey, Honeeeee, I'm outside with some very up tight assholesssss in suits."

Marie gets it, tells the boys she not dressed. By the time she finds the hash, they're banging on the door. She stuffs the shit in her bra, welcomes the detectives with a disarming smile that gets crushed when Owl Eyes strolls in at the back of the pack and says, "Bonjour, Marie." These two knew each other, he'd busted her for heroin years earlier. I could see Marie was scared. She would've felt a whole lot worse if she'd known there were still several grams of hash sitting on our tall dresser. I could see it, stuck just inside the only décor in the place, a dumb, Dutch clog.

The boys turn the bed over, check the closets, the oven, the fridge; they're looking for serious weight, but I know with six guys in small studio, it won't be long till one of them idly turns that clog upside down. I drift to the dresser, drape a loose arm in front of the drugs. With my other hand, I flick the wad deep into the shoe.

Marie tells them she needs to pee. They're French; they let her go alone. She waits a minute inside, then flushes what she thinks is our entire stash down the toilet. I'm on nice guy offense, languid at the dresser, warming up the crowd, defending the shoe. "Porsche and Volkswagen mechanic," I say in French. "Rallye Motors by the Negresco Hotel, been doing it for years, love this region, people are so nice here . . ."

It's not long til the posse runs out of things to check. They're looking at each other, an awkward silence. Maybe the kid doesn't have buried treasure, maybe he isn't a threat to France. Maybe, we've made a bad call?

"Okay, Monsieur," says the lead cop, "let's look at your Volkswagen."

*Fuck, what if another hippie who owned my ride, left some drugs under the seat?*

I keep the innocent chatter, hit the street, hand over my keys. The cops, hopeful again, turn the seats, inspect the engine compartment, knock on the walls and floor. Doesn't last long, and just like that, this squad, the power to end my life, huddles up, gives me a nod, walks away.

In the studio, Marie and I collapse in each other's arms, laughing about how lucky we've been. I call work, tell them I'm sick, we get high, make love, decide not to wait till the end of the month, not after this. We move a few miles East, to Villefranche-sur-Mer, another charming port town with narrow streets and alleys. Colorful, small restaurants line the promenade in front of the bay. Our new studio opens to a rooftop perch, a view along the coast for miles.

We are great together. Marie is light as a snowflake, at ease wherever we land. She's not possessive of my time, demanding of my emotions, ready to enjoy the moment without worrying about the future. We're gonna crew yachts around the world, so we start visiting Antibes, once a refuge for artists like Picasso, now heavy with boats and money. We party with the captains, hired to maintain yachts for owners who live in Paris, NY, and Palm Beach. We explore Provence, its isolated and ancient villages, cafes and bistros. The weather is perfect, so is our life, No one in Corsica knows where I am, but I think more and more about Sophie and Cara.

They have so little, no real income, living in our half-finished house. Cara is the casualty, but I can't go back, I can't. I was dying there, getting bitter, losing the fight. Years later, a therapist said, "No matter what Ian, you should have taken her with you." He was right, and when he said, it, I burst into tears. I didn't tell him that in France, it would have been felony kidnapping. (*l'enlèvement parental*) If I'd taken her out of the country, I would have been wanted on two continents and any arrest then would have sent me to jail and Cara back to her mother. All that's true, but I know I didn't find a solution because I didn't want one. I was thinking only of myself. I apologized to Cara for my behavior years ago, but I don't know if she will ever really forgive me.

In April, Marie and I are asked to deliver a classic Dutch canal boat from Arles, back to its home port in Amsterdam. We will go there via the inland canals of France. The *Mirabelle* is 60 feet long. She is flat bottomed, wide beamed, spacious and very comfortable. The owner, Jessica, a red headed matronly Brit with two pubescent daughters, needs a mechanic. Jessica is prickly, but not hard to get along with. Her daughters, fascinated by Marie and me, will take every opportunity to peer into the portholes of our cabin, especially if they think we might be making love. We'll take six weeks to go nine hundred miles, travelling the earliest commercial transportation system in Europe, an engineering miracle that in its time, unified the continent and delivered the Industrial Revolution.

The Canal du Midi will take us through remarkable country; from tiny villages to abandoned castles and grand homes. It's Cezanne's world. Oak trees, mulberries, and poplars line the canal. We'll pass vast fields of poppies, lavender, apple and peach orchards. Not thirty feet from our boat, families will picnic, old men fish. Children wave as we motor slowly by.

There are more than two hundred locks in the system ahead. I almost ended our trip, two hours after leaving Arles. At the first dock, there was a *commecant* already inside. The economic backbone of the canals, these 100-foot-long, mini-freighters are scaled down versions of an oil tanker. They have beautifully lacquered, wood superstructures at the rear which house the captain and his family in cozy comfort, leaving the entire front of the boat, some 80 feet, open for cargo, from wood to grain to coal.

We're next in line. I bring *Mirabelle* to shore, lash the bow to a tree. My crew goes below, leaving me on deck. The nearby lock begins to fill with water, the black hulled *commerçant* floats up, and the jaws of my immediate future open with the metallic groan of old gears. Finally, the barge exits, with the majesty of a locomotive. Water begins boiling to the shoreline from the force of the propeller, but I hold a professional, sailor's stance on deck; a cool dude, watching another Captain at work. That changes when I realize I, and therefore my boat, are moving.

*Mirabelle*'s stern, the part I hadn't bothered to tie to shore, is swinging out into the canal under the suction of the *commerçant's* whirling prop. Our mast, stepped and tied to the deck, extends fifteen feet behind us. It's already cleared the commercent's bow and is seconds from sweeping his car, parked on his deck, into the canal before continuing on to cut through the superstructure like a scythe. The unbelievable disaster is going down with the inevitability and measured pace of a coronation when I suddenly think, *Kick the transmission into forward. Max the throttle and drive the boat back to shore!*

I hit the trans, slam the gas and spin the wheel. Like Nureyev separating from Fonteyn in *Romeo and Juliet*, our mast, only a few feet from the guy's car, begins to swing back like a giant turnstile opening to let him pass. The captain and I exhale as one while my boat returns to shore. Order is restored.

The captain slumps over the wheel; his car, his boat, his life, all that was about to happen hadn't, and since his woman and mine were below deck, the near debacle is our secret. The guy, however, gets a second wind, goes righteous on me. First, he blasts his air horn repeatedly, then delivers what the French ironically call, "The arm of honor." He laid his left hand in the crook of his right arm and pushed his right fist in the air like a prizefighter throwing an uppercut, all while yelling a string of choice words in my direction which happily, I couldn't hear. As he sailed away, my crew clambered topside to find out why the boat had moved so suddenly. They got an edited version, but when we entered the next few locks, Jessica, the owner, stayed topside with a baleful eye.

All traffic comes to a halt at sunset on the canals, so wherever you are, you've arrived. Each night, we tie up to a tree – bow and stern – break out two bicycles and take small roads across green fields to the nearest town for milk, cheese, and eggs. Our nights are quiet, we feel a thousand miles from any other reality. In the next weeks, we cross elevated locks built atop Roman viaducts, seventy-five feet in the air, we traverse the Fonserranes, a world famous, seven-lock staircase, built in the 1600's. At the Arzviller tunnel, our boat will wait with a string of twenty others, to pass single file, through a mountain whose ten-mile passage, blasted out with dynamite a hundred years before, is only wide enough for one-way traffic. It is idyllic, but not without additional dangers. One day, we are motoring up the Rhone river. The spring runoff has swollen the flow to a torrent. At full throttle, we are just making headway. If the engine quits or we turn a few degrees to port or starboard, we'd have spun around, lost all control, and been thrown against the rocks. Once, a line tied to a very high lock got wrapped around my leg as we being lowered. I just got out of the loop before it would have snapped a bone. Several foggy mornings were spent on the bow, staring into the mist and blowing a horn every thirty seconds, hoping everyone else in our area was doing the same. Eventually, we took the River Seine into Paris, docked at the RAC center, Place De La Concorde, and spent four lazy days, wandering the city before motoring across Belgium, the North Sea and finally, to Amsterdam. Paid off, nowhere to be, no plan, no one to report too, we decide to hitchhike back to Paris and live there.

We move in with Marie's sister, Christine. Her small, fifth floor, one bedroom apartment near the Arc de Triomphe, had two lovely, large windows opening on a courtyard. We slept in an alcove facing the tiny kitchen. Christine's elegant building was one of hundreds designed by Baron Georges-Eugène Haussmann, every one of them, mirroring the dimensions of the street they bordered, which is why none were more than six stories high. He built spacious interiors, elevated ceilings, elaborate detailing inside and out. These upscale residences reflected the affluence of their inhabitants, the spirit of luxury. They also reflected Napoleon's will. He'd ordered Haussmann to rebuild Paris while still giving the city space for light and air.

Napoleon could do that; he had unlimited power. He'd taken over a feudal, bankrupt country and unified it with an army of bureaucrats who instituted top-down control via pens and paperwork. He centralized finances, politics, the entire operating structure of France so that everything and everyone reported to Paris, to him, to the big house; a thing of beauty for the man who made himself Emperor for life and whose reign lasted less than ten years before the French sent him packing into exile and ignominy. With 'Napo' gone, France put away the Corsican's portraits but not his tight-fisted control over the proletariat.

The new ruling class, which was really the old ruling class, papered the walls with a promise of democracy but they kept the money and power for themselves. They kept Haussmann's architecture for themselves too, bought his buildings and protected his layouts, especially in the tony, fifteenth and sixteenth *arrondisment*, where Christine now lived.

I began to explore Paris again, walking from the quiet streets of Saint Germain to the home of Paris' working class at Les Lilas. I wandered through gritty, energetic, Bastille. Every sector, or arrondisment, had its unique character and yet, each one was, as I would come to understand, wholly French; its people, both welcoming and insular and careful and above all, committed to the constancy of their life, the way they'd lived for centuries.

After a year in Corsica, a winter in Nice, I'd become a bi-lingual American at a time when few Parisians spoke English, and even fewer Americans spoke French. I would sometimes dream in French or find myself thinking in my adopted language. My easy fluency made the city both generous and indulgent. My accent and occasional gaffs were deemed charming. I once walked into a store to ask for a bag and instead, told the lady inside, she was an old bag. She got it right away, laughed and said my apology was all she needed.

Once, as we sat down to lunch with Marie's sister, Christine. A triangular tranche of Camembert cheese was passed to me. I cut off the very tip. Marie told me afterward, "Never take the tip, Ian, it's the best part, and impolite to take it for yourself." I had experiences like that all the time; small, but important insights into the culture of my adopted country. I soon knew why their handshake was soft. ("You're welcome here, but not yet trusted."), Why they never ask personal questions, (Everyone in France has a secret.) insisted that criticism be delivered between the lines. (In a time of monarchs and lords, a few wrong words could get you beheaded.)

## LET LOUCHE IN PARIS

At a dinner party one night, I sat next to Paul Luis Gastaud, an electronics designer who created Disco lighting, electrically controlled waterfalls and secret controls to open, close, or run anything from doors to rooftops. He provided enough toggles and switches to let clients think they controlled their universe; it made him rich. Paul, thick black hair, quick with a joke, compulsive and childlike, loved the idea of having an American around. He hired me to do "cablage," simple wiring, but soon saw I liked solving problems, a character trait that was not, *tres Francaise*. That quality set me apart and made me useful in his world of custom builds. Paul Luis would call me in, hand off a wad of cash, a ticket to Lisbon, Madrid, or Cannes and send me there to solve an issue. His final words, "De merde toi," "You're on your own." I loved it. PLG also had a growing contract with the King of Morocco and began sending me there; my first time back since I'd pulled out of Tangier with nothing more than the clothes on my back. In my newest iteration, I found a great work/life balance there. It's not hard when you have a document that says you are, "In The Service of the Royal Palace." Get pulled over after racing through a village in Gastaud's Ferrari at 110 mph, face a civil servant scheduling twelve months for a telephone, walk into a crowded hospital or a full restaurant, and that piece of paper will cleanse the system of all viscosity.

One time, I was tasked to fly to Rabat and ensure that His Majesty got solid radio reception from France. This was before satellite communications, so it was going to be an analog solution. Need a sixty-foot tower erected on the city's tallest building? Permission granted overnight; no need for engineering, environmental or safety permits. Want to run an underground cable from that tower to His Majesty's royal palace, a mile away? A company of Army Engineers will show up in the morning. The mission completes in a week, reception is assured, His Majesty is pleased and Paul Luis Gastaud becomes king of comms in Morocco. I travelled the country like a prince, explored Royal Palaces and private grounds, even got gossip about the King, his habits, his many wives, their jealousies, the isolation; the intrigue and politics of royal power.

At another dinner party in Paris, we met Amanda Rothschild. Amanda, 35, thin, graceful, an easy smile, embodied the unorthodox characters who lived in Paris; no judgment, no boundaries. For me, it was a big part of what made the city so exciting. Amanda, in keeping with the French love of lost causes, had married a revolutionary leader during the Algerian war and spent much of her considerable inheritance funding his battalion of rebels, fighting French colonialism. Her husband eventually died in battle and the widow Rothschild returned to Paris with her ten-year-old daughter, bought a four-bedroom walk up in Le Marais and kept her Algerian name on the door. Amanda's flat was open at all hours to a crowd of wanderers and lovers. She was down to earth, not fussy or stuck up.

All that changed the night we packed half a dozen people in my Renault 4L to have dinner in Saint Germain. Next to me on the front seat was Xanthe Carpenter, a girl whose artist father, Joe Carpenter, had been chased from the U.S. in the 1950's, during America's Red Scare. (the same one Carl Bernstein got caught up in.) The Carpenter family landed in Brazil and eventually emigrated to Paris. "X", as I called her, became a weaver of rugs, and trouble. She toyed with people, created social experiments, provoked incidents just to see what would happen.

During the drive that night, Amanda made an offhand comment about her current boyfriend, James, a black American from Chicago, possibly being unfaithful. This was Paris, Jimmy's playtime wasn't a stretch, but X saw an opportunity, because she had, in fact, slept with him only a few weeks before. I knew this because I'd been at her place that night, competed with James til 2AM, for the right to fuck her, and lost. She would have been fine with either one of us, she just wanted to watch it play out. Now, seeing the excitement in X's eyes, I stared at her intently. *Don't. Please don't...*

She did, which was bad enough, but confessing in a car with five other people made it a whole lot worse. In one second, Amanda transformed into the original version of herself; private schools, Rolls Royce's, cooks, servants; privilege at every level.

"Stop this car!" Commanded the Queen, a voice like a lightning strike.

I pulled over.

"Xanthe, out!" she said,

X opened her mouth to make things worse, but Anna had the floor, her command was final.

"Out of this car! Now!"

No one said a word. We kept our eyes straight ahead. X, crestfallen over her plan's short lifespan, got out, went home, and never returned to the playhouse. I visited Amanda a week later. She and James were on the sofa. It was France after all.

One day, I got a call from Chuck, a jazz drummer whose VW, I worked on. Chuck had a gig in Belgium with some trumpet player, wanted to know if I would drive him and his kit there. I owned a BMW 2002, was waffling about it until he told me we'd sleep at a famous house, known in the Jazz world as, 'The Pharmacy.' Its owner, a jazz fanatic, ran a legit drugstore and made his pharmacological reserves available to the musicians who stayed with him. Turned out, the trumpet player we were meeting was Chet Baker, second only to Miles Davis in reputation and visibility, worldwide. Chet, chiseled, handsome, was into heroin, so he was down with our digs. We hung out, had dinner, talked about Paris and New York, and around midnight, I heard the honey sweet sound of his trumpet in a living room rehearsal and an improv that went on for hours.

The next evening, I took Chet and Chuck to the venue. A great gig, standing ovation, but for some reason, Chet didn't have the money to pay full wages to his band. My guy was okay, but the bass player lost his mind, lost the argument too, when Chet punched him out. Chuck was supposed to continue to Italy with the group but the fight, and the prospect of not getting paid, led to a change of plans, Chuck took the return trip with me to Paris.

Marie and I were not only a French, American couple, we were pretty together. People invited us into their world. We travelled all over France, thanks to Gastaud, but I was often short on money. Beside the unpredictable jobs with Paul, I fixed cars on the street, sold a few as well, took odd jobs in construction and trafficked in hash. I was sending money to Sophie by then, sent a car too, when she needed one. Eventually, I visited Corsica, though Sophie had Cara stay with friends the first few times I came. That was hard for me. Marie of course, wanted to know if I slept with Sophie when I was there. I lied, told her "No." Marie said it didn't really matter because in some ways, I hadn't left my wife. She wasn't wrong.

Life with Marie was getting more complicated. Her sister Christine, blond, pretty, super sweet and accommodating, was a working girl, introduced to the life via one of France's biggest pop music producers, Claude Carrere. This guy was so busy selling musical bubble gum he only had time for one-night stands, which went to his fantasy of never seeing the same woman twice. That rule led his procuress far afield and one day, a proposal came Christine's way. She did the math; more money earned in two hours than she made in a week as a receptionist. He was famous, he was safe, she signed on, they made love. At the door was an envelope marked, "Pour les fleurs." (For the flowers.) Christine quit her day job, brewed up a clientele of diplomats, dentists and middle-class men who believed that "Liberté, égalité, fraternité" meant keeping the family together while having a 'petite amie' on the side. Wives too, often went in search of their own lovers, which gave the entire cultural zeitgeist enterprise a democratic patina.

Christine suggested Marie might meet Carrere. She asked me, hoping I'm sure, I would say, "No," but I didn't. I couldn't. The last thing I wanted was someone else counting on me, not in the glare of my rising guilt over abandoning my daughter for a cool life in Paris. Marie took her night with Carrere. She began to share Christine's clients, then got her own, though sometimes, men wanted to watch the sisters make love together. I would often wait in the spare bedroom in case there was a problem, and sometimes I'd jerk off when my girlfriend was fucking another man. She never got after me over her work but she was, I'm sure, grievously unhappy that I did nothing to stop her selling her body.

I had an incredible run in Paris; an adventure beyond anything I imagined, I was fluent, proud of being part of this wonderful city and its culture. I loved waking every day not knowing what would unfold, living from one minute to the next. But I was turning thirty. What I call, The DNA Surprise, was coming on; the one that suddenly pushes us out of our childhood and makes us want to belong, do something that matters. Above all, I was fed up being an illegal immigrant, knowing a twist of fate on any day, could upended my life and send me back to the US in cuffs.

One night, I drove to Mother's, a bar in Les Halles, to meet friends. I smoked a joint, then began looking for a parking place. I came around a random corner. In front of me was a line of CRS cops. (France's version of State Police.) doing one of their unannounced exercises; stopping every car coming down a single street and asking for papers, insurance and ID. My car reeked of pot, but I couldn't, back up or make a 'U' turn without triggering a car chase. I had no choice but to go forward. It just turned out that every cop on that gauntlet already had a car pulled over. I didn't breathe, stared straight ahead while each uniform glanced my way, assuming I'd get stopped by someone down the line. I drove through that minefield, passed every one of them. When I got home I had to shower off the sweat.

Our fracturing relationship came to head when Marie, who'd been flirting for months with an American singer in a rock band, finally said she had to make love with him to find out. I don't know why, but I took her to his apartment myself. Maybe I wanted her to think I didn't care, but when it happened, it hurt. I walked along the Seine for hours, sat down near the Pont de l'Alma, watching the river, the boats gliding past, crammed with summer tourists. A black-haired woman my age walked by, holding the hand of her young daughter, her eyes bright with joy over their day together. The woman smiled at me. I watched the little girl skip happily over the cobblestones paving the river walk, her pink skirt swinging like a church bell each time she jumped from side to side. I wondered how long her mother could keep her innocent.

I thought of Cara. I was tortured with confusion and regret. I'd escaped a prison sentence eight years before, made my way here against all odds, built this crazy, extraordinary life. The highs and lows since, had made me a man. It was time to live like one, time to clean up the mess I'd left behind.

# 13
# THE RETURN

"Fasten your seatbelts, please. We'll be landing at Philadelphia International shortly."

Cara and I peer out the window as our jet descends over Connecticut's summer hazed highways and rivers, towns large and small, the stuff of any landscape. But spackled across this one are a unique, American signature; dozens of baseball diamonds, their immutable geometry etched in the earth like religious symbols.

Cara's excited, "Where are we going to live, Dad? What school will I go to? Will I have friends?" Anxiety is percolating in my stomach; should I warn her there may be trouble ahead? Mom and dad, meeting us at the airport, think I'll walk through customs after all this time. We'll know soon enough.

It's Sunday afternoon. Immigration lines will be long, the officers in a hurry. There's a chance I might get through because checking passports on those computers is still a manual process, agent's option. I go with a middle-aged man, ill-fitting uniform, thinning hair, retirement's his career goal. I keep a low-key vibe as my gatekeeper starts a fast flip through my passport but slows over the dozen pages of colored stamps, dates that go back years. He looks me up and down, meticulously types in the numbers. His screen begins to fill, their side of the story. Gatekeeper's mouth drops. I lean in. "Don't panic," I say. "I'm here to take care of this. What do you want me to do?" He sees I'm solid, picks up a phone.

Cara's staring, wide eyed; she's five, but she knows what awkward looks like. "Sweetheart, there's a problem with my passport. I have to go talk to some people about it. Your grandparents are just outside those doors. If I don't come back right away, go with them. I promise, I'll see you later." Tears run down her cheeks. She doesn't know my mom and dad. *I should have told her. I should have gotten her ready for this!*

Two airport cops are fast walking my way. They put hands on me, everyone nearby is staring. "This is my daughter." I tell them. "Our family are outside the exit doors, name is Jarvis. Please, get her to them as fast as possible, do you understand?" They nod, but they have no idea what to do. Cara is trembling. "Daddy, don't leave ..." She pleads.

"Please don't worry" I say, and move to hug her, but the cops hold me back "I'm just gonna talk to these guys," I tell her. 'I'll be back soon. I love you, please don't worry."

That's all I get, They walk me to a windowless room, a few filing cabinets and desks, where I'm handcuffed to a water pipe. Twenty minutes later, the first Federal shows, mid-thirties, pistoled up, black T- shirt, a red FBI cap. He's pissed, all attitude, leaves me hooked to the pipe, takes the rent-a-cops outside. Two more agents arrive, join the huddle at the door. The uniforms leave, lead boy brings his crew in, pats me down, takes off the cuffs and makes it official. "Ian Eric Jarvis, you are under arrest for conspiracy to import fifty pounds of hashish in contravention of ... blah, blah, blah." One guy opens a cabinet, pulls out a tape recorder and turns it on. The other leaves the room, "Gonna telex Interpol and D.C," he says with a smug smile. "See what this guy's been up to ..."

Lead Boy looks over a thin file, puts his feet on the desk. "Anything to say?" he asks. Opening move, let the perp set the table. I'm a citizen here, I've got rights, can say I'm innocent, want a trial, make the government spend millions proving I'm full of shit. But I'm not gonna do that. My plan is a full confession; no lawyers, no waiting in line. I'm pleading guilty because it'll take the FBI, and the Prosecution, out of the game. I'm going with guilty because it sends me straight to a Federal Judge for sentencing, one on one, he and I, and nothing will flatter the high priest more than this initiate's humble request to step up and take the cure.

A confession also gives me creative control over my story. I'm not telling the court I was an illegal immigrant, drug merchant, car thief, part time pimp, all around outlaw, a millimeter from jail a dozen times. They'll get the sanitized version; straight work, straight life, good marriage, father to a daughter and two stepchildren; names, dates, and places, all knitted and seamless. I'm betting there's no trail in Europe. I'm betting I can scrape the scaly stuff off my dossier. I'm betting I'll be hard to hate.

"Look," I say. "I was involved in that drug deal, but I've been in Europe the whole time. I didn't know there was a warrant out on me. If those guys were arrested, okay, I'm not going to fight this."

Lead Boy looks at the second guy. "Yeah, I got it.", he says.

All in now, no going back. If I pull this off, score a break, I'll be late out of the growing up gate, but not too late. If I lose, if there is prison time – and I'm hard as nails about this – I'll find out what I'm made of.

Soon, return telexes begin coming in, the boys scan for arrests, warrants, illegal activity, but there isn't any. I answer questions, timelines mostly. A lot of what I say is true, it's just not the truth, but body language and voices begin to change, the threat level's going down. An hour later, the last answers come in from France and Spain: no mastermind there, no associates, not a scent of my real life. We're sitting around the campfire now, me telling story, spinning silk.

When the audition's over, they say I'll spend my first night in America at the Roundhouse jail, downtown Philly. I'll appear for a bail hearing tomorrow morning. "That place is bad," they tell me. "You're Federal, we'll get your own cell, you won't have any assholes to deal with." *Well hot damn. I have friends at the FBI.*

I'm cuffed, perp walked down the wide steps at Philadelphia International, an agent on either side. It's sunset; they wear cool shades. At the Roundhouse, in a gray, cinderblock room, papers are signed, my guys say goodbye. The Philly cops take a mug shot, fingerprints, valuables. (I tried to get those pics, fascinated to see who was staring into the camera that night. I was too late; the files were gone.) A jailer takes me underground, past rows of cells stinking of broken toilets, unwashed bodies, old food. Defeat fills this place like smoke. Men stand at the bars, feral, bored, watching the new guy get a single room. The door slams on my green painted, stone walled, 10' x 10' cell. People's initials, numbers and names, are scratched on the walls, some with dates running years back.

On the steel shelf where I'll bed down, there's one more gift from the management; two mattresses, so black with dirt they shine like graphite. I'll be happy to sleep between them. It's August, but this place is fucking cold. Cacophony here, voices explode. One guy keeps it up all night. "Turnkey, Turnkey," he screams. "I'm sick, get me outta here, Turnkey. I'm sick I tell ya', get me to a hospital!" I review my every move, all vibes, stay steady on the story. If I drop one line, the whole thing caves. At 9:00 AM, they take me to a holding cell with six other men, all innocent, just ask them.

Thanks to dad's late-night flip through the yellow pages, my defense team is a fifty-year-old ambulance chaser, his cheap, blue suit bejeweled by the metal screen between us, its tiny mesh pixilating everything on the other side. The lawyer's a lowlife, but he's my lowlife, tells me Cara spent the night with mom and dad. Huge relief, she's safe, all that matters.

My parents are in court. Cara has new clothes and a haircut. We give each other big smiles, a small wave. If she doesn't know why I'm here she's about to find out. The prosecution makes their drug kingpin case, wrap it up with, "Given his history your honor, eight years as a fugitive, we believe the defendant is a serious flight risk. We ask the court to hold him here until trial." My stomach turns on that one; six months in crazy land. The judge listens intently while my crack lawyer tells the court his client will plead guilty, has had no further transgressions during his eight-years as a fugitive. He points to my parents and Cara; says I have responsibilities to her and will be living with them. The judge looks me over,

"Mr. Jarvis returned to the U.S. voluntarily?" he asks the prosecution.

"Yes, Your Honor."

"He didn't try to hide his identity?"

"No, he did not."

"And I presume you have this flight risk's passport."

"Yes sir."

"Right. Bail is set at $50,000. Next!"

Dad puts 10 percent down; I'm on the street in an hour. It's hot and humid, the air ripe with the smell of uncollected garbage. I want to shower, get out of these clothes but we walk a few blocks for breakfast instead. I pull Cara aside and apologize. She, mistress of calm, says, "It's okay, Dad." I hold her hand, tell her we'll get this right, but I know I've put a bullet in her trust. At the restaurant, my mother asks why I'm pleading guilty. "We can beat this," she says. "I know people. We'll get your story in the papers . . . !"

She wants to take over, did it to my brother when he set out to beat the draft as a Conscientious Objector. Did it to my sister, Freya when she filed for divorce. Mom told them how lucky they were to have her, then escalated their shit beyond all reason.

"I'm not gonna play some game. Not gonna spend two years and fifty thousand dollars waiting for a decision. This plan, you can't be involved."

My job, burnish the narrative, one story, one thru line, something the system doesn't see every day: a felon already on the path of righteousness, a working stiff, loving father, payer of taxes. First, I need a job. Three days after making bail, I'm hired as a VW mechanic at Delran Motors, Delran NJ. In Europe, they wanted an American trained mechanic. In the U.S., they're impressed with a European. I get top wage, five dollars an hour, then borrow money from Dad to buy a big, red, Snap-On rolling toolbox. Inside, are just a few basic tools, but I make the right impression.

Delran's small, concrete, garage on Route 30, has four bays, a real cast of characters; Jimmy Wong, thick accent, just out of China, he laughs easily, Al Webster, bearded hippy, living an alt lifestyle and Billy, the owner's, long haired, teenage son, always pissed about something, maybe it's working for his father, Hank. I don't tell anyone I might be in prison by January.

The pretrial system starts up. Probation gets first crack. Their opinion over the next months will guide the judge. Thanks to Delran, I have a rare treat for them; full time employment. They don't give anything up in the meeting though, no smiles, not a friendly word, they've heard it all before. I stick to the story, cloak myself in humility.

I fire the asshole lawyer. Don't need him playing angles and running up the tab. Class act, he refuses to return the $5K retainer my Dad gave him. I meet blond haired, blue blood, Jock Hannum III, ex-Viet Nam marine. He spent the last five years as a Philadelphia prosecutor, will one day be Assistant AG for the state. His father was a lawyer, now a judge. Jock's just started out on his own, the system knows him, would be happy to see their guy get a win. He's a good person, smart, hardworking, straight as an arrow. He has a wonderful habit of saying, "Okay, let me repeat back to you, what I think you're telling about your case." He's perfect – the mirror image of my rehabilitation.

Our home life in Cherry Hill sucks. I don't want to live with my parents, bedding down in the spare room with Cara. She needs better, needs to see us doing better too. I rent a studio in the same building, Towers of Windsor Park. I do everything I can. I'm even handed, consistent, I cook, clean, solve problems, create stability, first time in years for both of us. But the best part of me is out of reach, my childhood dogging me all the way. I didn't know how to build the kind of trust where she could have shared her pain. She protected herself by always showing up bright eyed and ready to go. I buy it, but failing your children leaves a bill to pay; we are good, we are getting strong, but I may be destined to never have her forgiveness.

Cara starts public school. A month later my wife flies in to join her husband and child. Joanne and Steven, my stepchildren, follow soon after. I hadn't questioned Sophie when she turned Cara over in Corsica. I was just happy that she agreed. Now it all made sense. I'm supporting the tribe again, last thing I wanted, but this time it's not chaotic or emotional; everyone's waiting for my court date, January 12, and right now, having a family puts another gold star on my dossier. When Social Services visits us at the apartment, it only confirms our solid group. It's a pretty good story; other than the fact I'm fucking my boss's wife.

Alexandria is pretty, upbeat, black haired and pert. Her husband, Hank, a man's man, wears cowboy boots, lived in Alaska, shot a moose. Alexandria sometimes joins him to do paperwork at the office. One night, Hank gets tied up, Alexandria comes to cash out, tells me turning off the lights in the back room scares her. It's not like I hadn't noticed her measuring me up, but no way she was screwing one of the mechanics, and not on a dirty floor between greasy transmissions and dead motors. She solved the problem by bending over. I didn't know she was sexually compulsive, had even screwed her husband's son, Billy, which went a long way to explaining why he was so pissed off.

Two weeks later, I was made Service Advisor, "To give Hank some time off." She said. It's a tribute to his monumental ego that he never saw it. If he'd found out, he'd have beat the shit out of me, then fired my ass, not a great look for a guy on bail, and I would have deserved it for being that stupid.

Jock and I meet early the day of the trial. I'm wearing a gray, $50, three-piece suit. "Ian," He says. "I don't know which way this will end. You're sure you want to go through with it, the guilty plea? It's not too late to change your mind."

"I've had a long time to get ready, Jock."

"Well, if it goes badly, I'll ask for two weeks so you can put everything in order."

That gets me. I was 21 when I decided to cure the money question with a drug deal; a choice that was thoughtless, unconscious, and it drove the next decade. My decision to return six months ago is playing out today. One way or another, the next hour will drive the next decade. I'm good. I want a place at the table, turn my skills into resources, not tools of survival but either way, there's clarity, a path. I don't care if it's hard, just let me plant my feet, somewhere.

I think about what the family will face if I'm put away. Amazingly, we never talked about it. Everyone's here, my parents, Sophie and the kids. We enter the Federal Courthouse, a huge, somber, wood-paneled room with Greek columns and paintings of great Americans. The judge appears, goes to his pulpit, which looks to me like it's two stories high. He's tall, gray tipped beard, black robes, fifty or so, intelligent, which is all I want. Until now, he only knows what others have told him. He checks me out.

The clerk announces, "United States versus Ian Eric Jarvis." and reads the charges.

"Mr. Jarvis," the Judge says. "How do you plead?"

"Guilty, Your Honor."

"You stand before the court accused of a crime for which you have stated, you wish to plead guilty. That means I will make the final determination, at this time, in this court. Before proceeding, the court needs you to answer the following questions with, 'YES' or a 'NO.'"

- "Do you admit the conduct made and that it is punishable by the law?"

"Yes, Your Honor."

- "Do you admit and understand the charges?"

"Yes, Your Honor."

- "Do you know the consequences of the plea, both the sentence as it stands, and the possible sentences that could be given if you, the defendant were to have a trial?"

"Yes, Your Honor."

- "Do you know and understand the rights you are waiving by pleading guilty, including the right to counsel if unrepresented?"

"Yes, Your Honor."

- "The right to a jury trial?"

"Yes, Your Honor."
- "The right not to incriminate yourself? "

"Yes, Your Honor."
- "The right to confront and cross-examine your accusers?"

"Yes, Your Honor."
- "The right to appeal?"

"Yes, Your Honor."

He leans back in his chair. "That is all for now, Mr Jarvis, you can sit down. The trial may begin. Is there a statement from the Government?"

The Prosecutor reviews the bust in mind-numbing detail. I focus on every word, all nuance. They cover my escape, eight years as a fugitive, the shipment, its street value; "Millions," they say, and wrap it by telling the judge that the five other co-conspirators received a sentence of seven years, so the court must allocate equal sentencing.

The judge slowly swivels our way. "Mister Hannum. Your statement." Jock tells him the shiny version; young kid, one bad decision. Reminds the court I returned voluntarily, no additional crimes in that time, solid citizen in Europe, is married, has children, taking care of four people, family all in court, and working since he made bail, been promoted, hasn't missed a meeting or a date.

"Mr. Jarvis, do you have anything to add."

"Your Honor, I did this, this, thoughtless mistake. I was twenty-one. I've done my best to make good since then. If the court is lenient, I won't let you down,"

The judge nods, surveys the room, says. "If there is nothing further, I will pass judgment."

I stand, hands on the table to steady me up. He takes a minute, sorts his papers. Leans into the microphone.

"The defendant has admitted his guilt. He has also demonstrated remorse, not committed further crimes and has entered the social structure, taking care of his family, working diligently, becoming a part of his community. The prior defendants in this case received long sentences but today, fifty pounds of hashish pales in comparison to the kinds and quantities of drugs this court is seeing. The sentence given nine years ago would be out of range with our present standards. I hereby order three years, Federal Probation. This case is closed."

Tears flood my face. I came to surrender, they've given me license to live. I turn to find Cara, she bursts through, jumps in my arms. That spring, I will quit my job at Delran, begin buying and selling cars on my own. I will run so many ads in the local paper, the state comes after me as an un-licensed car dealer. In September, we'll drive as a family to LA, where, facing the same mountain of crap that always came with this marriage, I shamelessly abandon them again, and move to NYC. I'll only see Cara a few times in the next three years, but I will be relentless about rebuilding my life, believing that one day, I'll rebuild hers, too.

# 14
# DELIVERANCE

I'm back In Detroit after five days on the road. A downpour has flushed away the swamp of rotted leaves on my street, a service the city can no longer afford. I feel good, it'll be a quiet weekend. I open a cold beer, throw wood on the fireplace, light it up and turn on Star Trek; Spock is mind melding with Pike. Then the phone rings. "Oh helloooooo!" says Sophie. "So glad you're iiiiiin!"

*Fuck me,* I thought, muting the TV. *At least fifteen minutes till she gets to the point.* Her monologue would start with a rundown on the good life in LA. A syrup of New Age sound bites about diet or meditation, was sure to follow, then some heartfelt support about, "Getting your life together." When I was sufficiently numbed, the wrap up would begin: a mini update on Cara—all I really cared about—and finally, finally, She'd tell me what she really wanted.

I'd just moved to the Motor City for Smerling Imports, a New York company that made a fortune in the 70's with the platform shoe; glam gear, whose eight-inch heels and three-inch soles were the cruelest footwear since the ball and chain. Smerling got lucky, fashionistas like Elton, Bowie, and Kiss wore them on stage, firing up an army of clueless kids to wobble across America's dance floors like aliens fighting gravity.

A decade later, Smerling, trendless again had tapped Hugh Hefner, who was broke, dialing for dollars, and licensing his hysterical logo on anything from eyeglasses to underwear. My new employer bet that Playboy's, chrome-plated Bunny medallions, screwed into the heel of every shoe, would turn their uninspired designs into a cash cow.

Problem was, Hef's air brushed blonds weren't titillating tone-deaf executives anymore. The only demographic at Playboy's trough was the working class, but in Michigan, the working class had no work. Detroit's three kings, the CEOs at Ford, Chevy, and Chrysler, had swapped quality for profits, then awarded themselves gold-plated retirement packages in case it didn't work out. The unions, swooning under the mantra that the good times would never end, pulled down the richest contracts in history while the Japanese, whose illusions about a new world order had been gutted by America's bombers in WW2, built new factories from scratch and figured out how to make better cars at half the price.

Any irony about Detroit's nosedive was lost on the region's newly welfared work force, stuck with gas guzzling American cars, and pocket change for the pump. Detroit's pawnshops, leading indicators in any recession, were wall-to-wall with golf clubs, outdoor barbeques, and used wedding rings. Worse, hundreds of families were torching their homes for the insurance just as the city was laying off its firemen – a match, some said - made in heaven.

Smerling had gifted me America's economic Siberia because I was a new hire, zero experience and by all estimates, least likely to succeed. I got the job thanks to Delta Airlines, who seated one-time girlfriend, Barbara Reno, next to Smerling's VP, Dick Goldstein, on a flight from Atlanta to New York. Dick was an aggressive little man, hiring staff for his hot, new footwear line. Barbara, channeling her "dear heart," southern charm, told him about the perfect candidate.

Then she called me with his number and said he was looking forward to our interview.

*What's that, Mr. Goldstein? A guy like me, don't know shit about shoes, never had a legit job, fired from a dozen Big Apple restaurants, what have I got to offer? Plenty. First, I got fired for attitude, not bad work. I wasn't hanging out after midnight when the only table in the joint was a bunch of satiated pricks too soiled with overpriced wine and the prospect of getting laid to pay their bill and take it home. With the blessing of the entire staff, I'd burn through their booze and cocaine with a cold stare and towering attitude, till they surrendered and called for the check. I'm ten times smarter than those guys, Mr. G, so why not hire an ex-federal felon? How much horsepower could you get from this pissed-off former outlaw, furious about serving soup du jour on Saturday night while everyone else my age is at play. Just give me a business card and a phone. I'll slay your elephant. I will kill for success.*

I dialed up Smerling's VP and referenced my friend. Goldstein was tough, rude, didn't remember her, told me to get to the point.

"I'm thirty years old." I said, "I speak three languages, and I can sell anything you make."

"Oh yeah? Maybe I ought to see you."

That's why I was in Detroit, earning $800 a week against the commissions I'd earn convincing shoe stores in a dead economy that thin-soled footwear featuring Playboy's logo was a breakthrough product. I didn't know a wing tip from a brogue, so I bought a few Bunnified air fresheners, license plate frames, and sunglasses, told Ma and Pa these best sellers from Playboy meant millions of American men were waiting for the next big thing from Hugh's sexy shop and Smerling was giving it to them; Playboy's tits and ass were gonna sell shoes. The pitch opened new stores, but it'd be a long time till sales commissions in the frozen zone would match a draw of $42K a year.

The post-war, red brick house I rented was in a working-class district near Fisher Highway. The previous tenant, left behind a wine-colored velvet sofa and flower print curtains. I rounded out the interior with a mattress and microwave from the Salvation Army. It looked like a college dorm. Didn't matter. I had a real job, a company car and regular hours, I'd sleep in Motel Six and eat at Burger King. I'd bang on doors in two horse towns like Ypsilanti, and Zanesville because one way or another, I would leverage this hard stop in the shoe business into a career, do something I could love, a life I could be proud of. That's why, on the night my ex-wife called, the last thing on my mind was that her goals and mine had aligned.

I was trying to lip read Captain Kirk's conversation with Uhuru, when Sophie knocked me out of my stupor with a clunky segue to a new boyfriend. *Why are you telling me this?* I thought. *And why would I give a damn when your idea of a great relationship is rough sex with a first aid kit nearby?* I was about to tell her I had to run to the bathroom and I'd call back later, when she said the words that changed my life.

"So, I was wondering ... could Cara stay with you for maybe, six months, so Zack and I can get to know each other better ... "

Holy shit. Did my ex-wife say she wanted to hand over our daughter? Is the gorilla on my back standing down? I was speechless, pinballing between hope and fear. "Absolutely want to do this," I said. "Completely understand how much in love you are but can it wait a bit because I'm on the road selling shoes five days a week and it would be hard to, I don't know, create stability for her. How about I change careers in no more than say, ninety days, then I'll come for Cara?"

"Are you telling me, no?" Sophie thundered. "You're a selfish pig! You've never done anything for her! This is something really kind on my part and you should jump at it!"

I'd been carrying our stones for years, so I took up the invitation.

We belched accusations, recrimination, rewrites of fact and fiction, and when I'd pulled enough memories off my crowded shelf to declare victory, I slammed the phone down with a sincere, "Fuck you!"

I was excited, my turn to screw with her. But a few minutes with a cold beer, a warm fire, the adrenaline drained. *Hell*, I thought, *Sophie's new wrestling partner won't last. Then she'll change her mind about sending Cara.* Sucking up all pride, I called back, only had to grovel a few minutes. She wanted this.

Forty-eight hours later I landed at LAX to re-father my eight-year-old daughter. The smiling little girl I hugged at the door had last spent serious time with me, half her lifetime ago. Her mom and I might have taken a few minutes to comfort Cara about this monumental change, explain why this was happening. There was none of that. Sophie, dealing with guilt and understandable concerns about my lifestyle, went right into a list of challenges about my plans and parenting skills. The slightest resistance, she would have thought something was up, lost her temper and sent me home. She'd have been right. In principle, this was a six-month loan-out, but I had no intention of returning Cara. I stayed humble, signed a promissory note, and got us on our way.

The flight to Chicago was a three-hour reality check. The first stage of my economic recovery was over; there was no alchemy that could fix this;. Cara had lived in chaos. She needed one address, one school, one world. There was no future here, not with me on the road all week. Even if I had to return to Vermont as a VW mechanic at $5 an hour, that would have to work. For now though, I had to stay with Smerling a month or two, to save a few bucks,

I held her hand while she slept, a tanned angel in a pretty print dress and sandals. There are circles under her green eyes. Dark, curly hair flowed down her shoulders. Was it DNA that made her feel she could trust this stranger? Was she still connected to the face that long ago leaned in to rock her crib, change her diapers, hold her when she cried? What would she say if she knew I didn't intend to send her back?

My house looked more like someone moving out than in, but both of us had lived like that before. The fridge was stocked, her room had a bed, a rug, and a dresser. After dinner, I tucked her in, kissed her goodnight, lit a fire in the living room and sat down to map our future.

At some point though, I felt her energy. I turned. The bedroom door was cracked open, Cara staring at me like a lost puppy. Without a word, she slowly backed up into the dark. These were my first hours parenting, I was dumb as a tree branch. But when she came to the door a second time, I got the message, went in, and asked, would she feel better if I slept in her room. Her relief was palpable. I dragged my mattress in, settled down. A few minutes later, I looked over. She was still staring, wide eyed, even though I was only feet away! I moved my mattress next to hers. We slept like that for weeks.

I didn't ask why, and that's on me. Knowing her life those years, I should have eased Cara into therapy once we got settled. We might have uncovered the events that skewered her childhood. She only told me about them in her twenties, after the PTSD boiled up. Cara had been deeply abused in so many ways, and like many children with no recourse, she'd become brave and self-sufficient way too soon, built her defenses to reveal nothing, appear happy and fool everyone around her. I was to do many things for her in the next few years, but I was blind to an important part of her story.

If I wanted to deliver a life for her, one of the first steps had to be education. Cara told me she hadn't been in a classroom for two years. I wasn't dropping my daughter into an underfunded, Detroit school, halfway through the semester. Beyond her classmate's rejection, the administration probably would have started her a grade behind.

We were leaving Detroit anyway, so I told the neighbors my

niece was staying with me for a month while her parents re-located to England. We hit the road; long car rides, rambling conversations, lots of attention. We ate at restaurants, slept in motels. Cara would help carry my sample bags into stores, then watch me sell. I found her incredibly mature. Too often, with Sophie, she'd become an adult in the room, taking care of her mother when she freaked out over bills, rent, or the men who came and went like hummingbirds.

By December, I had a thousand dollars; enough to move to Vermont and work as a mechanic again. It wasn't going to be much money, but she'd know where she lived, and she'd know it wasn't going to change on her. I was days from telling Smerling I was quitting, when a call came in from Janet Kerr, gifted pianist and friend from the Lower East Side of New York. We'd met because I owned a 1973 Chevrolet, a relic so big I made money after work, driving bands to gigs in the city. One of those groups was Janet's.

She had a day job, office manager for Pierre Dinand, the world's number one designer of fragrance bottles. Pierre's creations conveyed the sensual look and feel every brand needed to set itself apart on the crowded shelves at stores like Bloomingdales and Saks. In this esoteric niche, Pierre was a star; a track record of success with Obsession, Armani, Paco Rabanne, YSL, Balmain, Dior, and dozens more. He was at the top of his game, but it hadn't been easy. His breakthrough came thanks to Japanese designer, Kenzo, who, in 1977, asked Pierre to create a look for a major fragrance launch. After months of research, Dinand, presented a bottle based on the flask that Japanese Samurai carried into battle. Kenzo was offended, thought it diminished his worldwide brand, and fired Pierre. Kenzo went on to design his own bottle, called it King Kong, and took a three-million-dollar bath.

A short time later, Yves St Laurent approached Pierre for a new package. Pierre gracefully waited two months and then placed on St.

Laurent's table, the very same Samurai flask he'd given to Kenzo. St. Laurent loved it, bought the design, named it *Opium* and created one of the biggest successes in fragrance history. Off that design, Pierre became the industry's go-to designer, harnessing his presence and power in every direction. Months before I left for Detroit, Janet had said, "One day, the right job will come up in my industry. I'll set a meeting with Pierre now. If he likes you, we'll get an interview somewhere, when the timing's right."

Because Janet got me a ten-minute meeting with her boss, because I spoke French, and because sometimes, the cavalry does show up in time, four weeks after Cara's arrival closed out my life in footwear an angel, Janet Kerr, offered me up to perfume bottle maker, Saint Gobain; a $4 billion, French multinational who wanted a bi-lingual, sales ace to open the US market. It was an executive slot, a high-profile position, a game changing move to the big time, and no one was less qualified for it, than me.

Saint Gobain produced architectural and automotive glass. They'd expanded into pharmaceutical bottles a decade earlier and were already in the American market, selling those bottles to pharma majors for vaccines and aspirin. Now, the company had a new CEO in Paris, forty-year-old Vincent Bastien, who'd just bought a perfume bottle plant in Normandy called *Desjonqueres*. He wanted his Saint Gobain on the podium in the high quality, highly competitive, gloriously upscale, American fragrance industry.

Hiring SGD's first ever, perfume glass salesperson, fell to New York Pharmacy bottle President, Pascal Conille. Pascal's number one goal was not hiring anyone from France. He knew that New York companies would never put up with Euro arrogance, non-answers, and late deliveries. He also knew any French Sales Director would backdoor with the execs in Paris; the kind of intrigue Pascal didn't have time for.

He spent six months meeting bi-lingual Americans with good resumes and sales skills. Candidate after candidate failed the audition. They'd studied the language, read Sartre and Balzac, spent their junior year abroad, but no one understands the French unless they sleep with them, read their newspapers, and listen to infantile pop music and pontificating intellectuals. Understanding France means recognizing regional accents, knowing what really happened in Algeria, why the French prefer getting bad news between the lines.

With Pascal facing the awful prospect of hiring a Parisian, Pierre Dinand, who'd been circling like a hawk, gave Pascal a call. Pascal wanted to please Pierre, who could send million-bottle fragrance orders to any glass company he chose. Pierre, if he placed the new salesperson, would have an ally for his own maneuvers. It was a board game for them, but it was life and death to me. This job would exorcise a lost decade, put me in the winner's circle with a chance to make things right with my daughter. All I had to do was convince a three-hundred-year-old French institution – they'd made the mirrors in The Palace of Versailles, for God's sake – that an American felon with no proven sales record could open an entire country.

Pascal flew me in for a meet up at his small office on East 43rd St. The place was a dump, worn carpets and hospital green walls, okay for big Pharma, where aesthetics didn't matter. Pascal, early forties, had straight black hair, bright eyes, great energy. I made an ironic reference to the elevator stop I witnessed on the 12th floor, a gay bathhouse, swilling with disinfectant.

"Not the same fragrance" I said in French.

Pascal burst out laughing. We got along splendidly. he even told me about their retirement plan. I flew home to Cara, totally excited. Three days later, Pascal called. I heard the bad news in his voice as soon as he said, "Hello." He'd forwarded his notes and my resume to the top executives in France. One of them, Christian Marchandise, number three man at Saint Gobain, wasn't buying Pascal's opinion, or my resume.

Marchandise was right. Ex mechanic, ex-waiter, ex-Federal Felon, college dropout, new single parent, and Sales Manager for Playboy Footwear; not the look that would win this contest. I did what any felon would, I wiped my past, dumped my Playboy logo, and printed business cards making me Midwest Sales Director for Pierre Cardin Footwear. I created a two-state territory with three salesmen and a $250,000 P&L. The number on my new business card went to a red phone installed at a girlfriend's house. If it rang, she'd answer, "Pierre Cardin Footwear" and take a message for her boss, Mister Jarvis. I even called Paul Luis in France. He let me print PLG business cards to cover my years living with Marie and Christine, and committed to confirm my employment if Saint Gobain called.

In all, I wallpapered a decade. Marchandise smelled the con, asked to have me interviewed by NYC headhunter, Doug Mancini, who soon called, offering to visit Detroit and tour my "operation." Since I didn't have one, I proposed we meet in New York. Three days later, I flew in for a meeting at his plush offices, top floor view of the Empire state building. I was rattled, over my head, did not do well. He let me stumble through, but I knew I was cooked when he walked me to the door and said with a feline smile, "Be sure to get your air fare refunded from SGD."

He waited a respectful few days before submitting his thoroughly negative report. "I wouldn't be successful in a large enterprise," was how he put it. Pascal gave me the news, but I was ready with a rebuttal. "Pascal," I said. "Mancini's earning what, $2,000 for the interview? He cuts me out, comes on to S.G.D. for a full search and bills you $30K. Why would he give this candidate a green light?" That made sense to

Pascal. His visceral optimism still strong, he pulled a note together for Paris, suggesting I go there for an interview. The executives agreed. Pascal's last words as he handed me my tickets: "It's in your hands, Ian."

My meeting at the headquarters in the Paris suburb of La Defense, began with CEO, Vincent Bastien and VP, Paul Lugat. I'd left Georgetown University, my junior year. In France, that doesn't mean you were bored to death or interested in wider horizons; it means you are stupid, and almost certainly untrustworthy. I did not, as they say, have "Le bon profile." Bastien donated a few minutes. I didn't see him again.

Lunch with Lugat and a few minor dignitaries was next. In an inspired move to impress them with my French, I started using street slang; called a "voiture" a "bagnole" and referred to an individual as "mec." Who knew corporate culture didn't embrace that kind of informality at this stage? I was afloat on my ignorance, feeling good about my chances, right up to the moment Pierre Dinand, who had joined us at the table, leaned over as judiciously as one can in front of eight strangers and whispered, "Ian, speak in English."

What I couldn't know was my poor performance made me a jewel in the CEO's hands. He wanted to fire Marchandise; these two very intelligent men had no respect for each other. Bastien's move was to leave the hiring decision to Christian. If he rejected me, nothing lost. But if that idiot actually made the hire, he would get blamed when this uneducated kid who shouldn't have been there in the first place, blew a critical launch in the world's most important market. With that costly debacle, Bastien might bury his VP of Marketing.

I knew nothing of this when I met Christian, an extraordinary individual; intellectual and worldly, a big man with kind, brown eyes, and a huge dose of charm. He was my last chance. A little humility and understatement might have slipped me right into his French heart; all

I had to do was keep my mouth shut, look sincere and say one or two intelligent things. But I was afraid to appear unknowing and went too far. Stuff I hoped might impress, fell flat. I've no doubt the people he introduced me to, felt the same way.

We were together two days, seeing factories, executives, and managers. On our last night, with no one left to meet, we had dinner, one-on-one. When I mentioned having custody of my daughter, Christian leaned in, his energy changed. How had I gotten her? What was the daily stuff like, cooking, homework, discipline? How did Cara feel about not living with her mother? Did I think I would have a personal life? Did I take her to school every day and pick her up? For the first time, I could be honest, we made a connection, the only moment I had, but it was clear this personal conversation wouldn't change the outcome.

I was awake that night, coming to terms with the loss. In the morning I'd thank him for his time, act untroubled when he gave me a soft goodbye. *Whatever it takes, I'll make it somewhere* I thought. *Even if I have to start over in Vermont.* We made small talk at breakfast, then he called for the check, I held on to my pride, there was nothing left to do.

But at that moment, Christian Marchandise, a guy who knew the score, saw my weakness and inexperience, heard every opinion about why it was out of the question to hire me, this stranger, this SVP at global giant, Saint Gobain, pulled a napkin off the table and wrote on it, the terms of my employment.

I was going to launch their US division in New York. I would bring my daughter to a great city, join my peers, live right, have access to everything I'd hoped for. On the flight back, I kept pulling that napkin out of my pocket. *What happened back there? It doesn't make sense.* Months later when Christian and I had lunch in New York, he told me.

"First of all," he said, "you didn't do well in France, but it was clear to me, you were intelligent."

It had become personal for him over dinner, he said, because he was losing his two daughters in a custody battle. If I'd beat the odds to get Cara back, if I was bringing her up alone, taking responsibility to love, guide, and shelter her, Christian felt it was his business to give me a shot. I'd killed to get this opportunity; lied, cheated, and fought for it all the way, but my life was turned around by a simple act of fate that brought Christian's loss and my gain to the same constellation.

In April, I started work in SGD's new offices, at 600 Madison Avenue. Soon after, CEO, Vincent Bastien came to visit. As he was leaving, Mister Saint Gobain took me aside, put a hand on my shoulder and said, with a thoroughly insincere smile, "Ian, be sure to sell Estée Lauder. They are our most important client."

Lauder, the whale, the industry leader. Vincent had given impossible marching orders to a guy just out of the gate. The next week though, I called on Lauder's four purchasing directors. Three of them told me to go prove myself somewhere else, they weren't taking risks with an unknown. The last of the Big Four was a man named Tommy Sinatra, tall guy, eager eyes, big black mustache. Lauder only had two qualified glass suppliers and Tommy, recently hired, figured it would be useful for his career to successfully develop a new bottle resource when no other Lauder executive had the nerve.

We met for lunch at La Caravelle, near Park Avenue, not far from Lauder's corporate offices in the GM building. Based on the foundation of every great business relationship - temporarily matching agendas - he stepped up and put me on Lauder's supplier list. With Tommy's help, I navigated the technical hurdles and the politics, leapfrogged over issues that would have sidelined the process; learned everything on the fly. Ninety days after Vincent Bastien's throwdown, I faxed my CEO in Paris an Estee Lauder purchase order for one million bottles.

That breakthrough quashed all questions about the new hire. With Lauder in my column, I leveraged the industry, opened the market and made major sales across the country. Eighteen months after starting at Saint Gobain, I was named VP of the American division and began hiring staff to meet our growth. I was back on the rails of the American dream, in control of my life, the first time in a decade.

Cara, after a summer of one-on-one, professional tutoring, was academically up to speed and attending Birch Wathen, a private school on the upper east side. She'd found friends and a growing sense of confidence. We moved out of a mid-town studio to an uptown duplex, rented a summer house in the Hamptons. The only curse I had were the weekends. I couldn't wait to get back to work.

Vincent Bastian would have to fire Marchandise without me. And he did.

I would go on to a great career on New York and LA, bring up my daughter for ten years, sell my own company and then re-invent myself in writing, film, music and radio. That's another story.

www.ingramcontent.com/pod-product-compliance
Lightning Source LLC
Chambersburg PA
CBHW020053170426
43199CB00009B/264